8 VOCATIONAL PERSPECTIVES SERIES

E. F. O'Doherty, M.A., B.D., Ph.D.

VOCATION, FORMATION, CONSECRA-TION & VOWS

Theological and Psychological Considerations

alba house   A DIVISION OF THE SOCIETY OF ST. PAUL
STATEN ISLAND, NEW YORK 10314

157069

Current Printing (last digit):

9 8 7 6 5 4 3 2

Nihil Obstat
    Daniel V. Flynn, J.C.D.
    Censor Librorum

Imprimatur
    James P. Mahoney, V.G.
    Archdiocese of New York
    September 15, 1971

The nihil obstat and imprimatur are official declarations that a book or pamphlet is free of doctrinal or moral error. No implication is contained therein that those who have granted the nihil obstat and imprimatur agree with the contents, opinions or statements expressed.

Library of Congress Catalog Card Number: 76-110594

ISBN: 0-8189-0205-1

Designed, printed and bound in the U.S.A. by the Pauline Fathers and Brothers of the Society of St. Paul, 2187 Victory Blvd., Staten Island, N. Y. 10314 as part of their communications apostolate.

Religious life in our time has demonstrated its health and vigor by undergoing changes more profound and far-reaching in a decade than perhaps in the last few centuries. These profound changes cannot of course be changes in essence. They are the culmination of what Edmund Burke in another context has called "the slow organic growth of social institutions." These manifestations of growth, often correctly called adaptation after the model of evolutionary thinking, are the result of the devoted response of religious themselves to the request of Vatican II:

"The appropriate renewal of religious life involves two simultaneous processes: (1) a continuous return to the sources of all Christian life and to the original inspiration behind a given community and (2) an adjustment of the community to the changed conditions of the times."

"Communities should promote among their members a suitable awareness of contemporary human conditions and of the needs of the Church. For if their members can combine the burning zeal of an apostle with wise judgments, made in the light of faith, concerning the circumstances of the modern world, they will be able to come to the aid of men more effectively."

("Decree on the Appropriate Renewal of Religious Life." *Documents of Vatican II*, Association Press 1966, pp. 468-469)

The material which follows requires a word of apology, both in respect of content and of presentation. Although we speak about the vows, it will be seen that only two of them are dealt with in any detail: chastity and obedience. The reasons for the emphasis on chastity and obedience are first the demand from religious themselves for a treatment of these two, and secondly the fact that both are much more under fire than poverty at this time.

This volume is the result of the transcription from tapes of lectures, seminars and discussions with religious, held in many parts of the world. There is a big difference between a lecture to a live audience and a script written for the gifted reader's eye. Though the lectures have been edited, the critic will discover many faults of presentation and style, as well as inadequacies of content. For these faults I take complete responsibility.

My debt of gratitude to the Sisters whose enthusiasm and devotion made this book possible is incalculable.

E. F. O'Doherty

Foreword **v**

PART I: VOCATION 3

 1. Renewal and Relevance 3
   The Notion of Consecration 7

 2. The Theology of Vocation 13
   Psychological Fitness 19
   "Temporary" Vocation 21

PART II: FORMATION 25

 3. Grace and Human Personality 25
   A New Pelagianism 27
   Grace and Natural Perfection 31
   Confidence in Man 36

 4. Acts and Motives 41
   Behavior 41
   The Notion of Conduct 45
   Memory and Imagination 49
   Motivation 51

 5. Phases of Development 57
   Personality Differences 57
   The Notion of Character 60
   Stages of Maturation 61
   Self-Initiated Acts 65

6. The Psychology of Adolescence   69
   Self-Identity   69
   Role Learning   72
   Cultural Values   76

7. Emotional Maturity   79
   Control   79
   Responsibility   82
   Autonomy   83

8. Masculine-Feminine Psychology   89
   Unreal Stereotypes   89
   Masculine-Feminine Roles   92
   Social Status   93
   Psychological Differences   95

9. The Middle and Declining Years   101
   Senescence and Senility   101
   The Under-Thirty Generation   103
   Skills   106
   Emotional Life   108
   Fear of Death   111
   Problems of Old Age   113

PART III: THE THREE VOWS   117

10. An Overview   117
    Chastity   118
    Obedience   120
    Poverty   121

11. The Theology of Chastity   125
    Chastity — A Form of Loving   125
    The Vow and Virtue of Chastity   127

Eternal Generation of the Son   128
The Generation of the New Creature in
Baptism   128
The Incarnation   129
The Living Flesh   131
Chastity — A Way of Being Human   132

12. Psychosexual Development   135
    A Sacred Choice   135
    Finality   136
    Incommunicability of Human Love   137
    The Ordinariness of Sex   138
    Its Universality   139
    Developmental Aspects   140
        Infancy   140
        Childhood   141
        Puberty   144
        Adolescence   145
        Adult Desire   147

13. The Psychology of Chastity   151
    What to Expect   151
    Immature Personalities   152
    The Over-Concerned   153
    The Over-Repelled   155
    The Over-Attracted   159

14. Psychosexual Problems   161
    Masturbation   161
    Friendship   162
    Inadequate Ways of Handling Sexuality   166
        Repression   166
        Misreading Biological Processes   167

	Pain as Gratification	168
	Aggression	168
	Control	169
	Joy	170
15.	Obedience	173
	Conformity	174
	Constraint	175
	Free Choice	176
	Role of the Superior	178
	Problem of Reasonableness	181
16.	Conscience and Freedom	185
	Freedom	186
	The Formation of Conscience	188
	Constituents of Conscience	193
	Authority Roles	198
17.	Authority and Religious Life in Vatican II	203
	Role Definition	204
	Two Opposing Views	205
	The Document on Religious Freedom	208
	The Principle of Conscience	210
18.	"Subjects"	215
	Free Intelligent Beings	215
	Role of Leadership	217
	The Notion of Disobedience	220
	The Exercise of Authority	222
	Independence and Autonomy	224
	Growth in Obedience	226
19.	"Superiors"	229
	Dimensions of Authority	230

Fundamental Principles 232
Stereotyping and Rigidity 235
Authority Problems 237
The Exercise of Authority 240
Summary 242

20. The Disturbed Religious 245
The Art of Counselling 246
Psychiatric Problems 249
Personality Problems 256
Impersonal Conflicts 257
Morale 259
Spiritual Problems 262
Suggested Remedies 265

PART I: VOCATION

1. RENEWAL AND RELEVANCE

In the *Decree on the Appropriate Renewal of Religious Life* we read: "The appropriate renewal of the religious life involves two simultaneous processes: (1) a continuous return to the sources of all Christian life and to the original inspiration behind a given community; (2) an adjustment of the community to the changed conditions of the times." Further on we read: "Communities should promote among their members a suitable awareness of contemporary human conditions and the Church's needs." These contemporary conditions are our concern here.

The Decree clearly states the purpose of this return to an understanding of the human condition: "In such a way, judging current events wisely in the light of faith and burning with apostolic zeal, they may be able to assist men more effectively." This assistance must be seen in its perspective and we cannot understand the perspective of religious renewal unless we understand the essential concept of the theology of the lay apostolate.

Every document of Vatican II must be read in the light of the others, never in isolation. These documents define the lay apostolate as: "the participation in the saving mission of the Church itself." This mission is: "the restoration of all things in Christ and raising the whole world to a spiritual level." The Council teaches that the laity is called in a special way to make this mission present and operative in those places and circumstances where only through them can one become the "salt of the earth" (Mt 7:13). This teaching has shaken the morale of many religious. One problem demanding immediate solution is that of the religious' role in our contemporary world. Young people ask: "Why should I be a religious? What can I do as a religious that I cannot do as a lay person? If I were a teacher, preserving Christ's way of life, perhaps with consecrated virginity in the world, could I not do a better job?" This question is basic and unless we have a clear answer, it is useless to tackle any secondary question.

To give this answer we penetrate more deeply into the mystery of the Church to obtain a clearer understanding of the religious life. The Council teaches: "Christ the Lord abundantly blessed the many-faceted love (between spouses) welling up as it does from the foundation of divine love and structured as it is on the model of his union with the Church." Some facets of the "many-faceted" love of God for his Church have perhaps eluded us in the past, but we have come to understand them better since the Council.

First, there is is the concept of the theology of the elect. Election, as used scripturally, is a free and gratuitous act of God. We know that the whole human race was created and redeemed and this creation and redemption constitute the Christian's call to perfection. There is not another step during which the created and redeemed are called to perfection. In the case of religious, however, there is another call, another confrontation, over and above the call to Christian perfection.

Creation and redemption were for all mankind, but out of all mankind Israel was chosen as the People of God. The People of God are chosen and from them the multitude is chosen, our Lord taking pity on the multitude. Out of the multitude, the group, the thousands by the lakeside, are specially taken care of and taught by him. The seventy-two is a smaller group still, specially chosen and sent on a mission. The Twelve is another group, and out of the Twelve three are chosen, Peter, James, and John, to witness the Transfiguration and the Agony, and out of the three, John becomes the "beloved disciple." There is always a narrowing down and a gradual determination of a special vocation. The religious' vocation is that extra, over-and-above creation and redemption. The essential concept of this vocation is not the sacrificial element as this is the essential concept of the priesthood. The essential concept of the religious life is "consecration," the setting apart as sacred, the specially chosen of the Lord.

Parents, through the act of generation, give human nature to the child they conceive. Distinct from this is actual existence which can be of different kinds. First, through human generation a merely temporal existence is given since from a space-time creature all that can result lies in the space-time order. However, coinciding with this act of generation, God replaces this finite existence with an immortal existence through the infusion of a spiritual soul, every human being receiving this type of existence. But there is still a third type given through baptism whereby the person receives a supernatural existence, a real sharing in the divine life. This is not merely a superimposing on the previous type of existence, rather it is a total ontological change of the person. The baptized now possesses a divine mode of existence. In Pauline terms he is made a new creature: "Therefore, if anyone is in Christ, he is a new creation; the old has passed away, behold, the new has come" (2 Cor 5:17).

The third existence changes nothing in the physical, observable area; however, it does mean that everything the child does is transformed in its reality, meaning, and efficacy. Before being baptized, the child is living the existence communicated by the human soul, breathing, crying for food, smiling at his mother. After baptism, nothing changes in an observable way; he still breathes, eats, and smiles at his mother. All his actions which were already good and worshipful are now themselves worship and prayer because they are the actions of a Christian who shares in the life of grace. This means that their whole significance has changed. But this change is not observable in the physical order; it is strictly a matter of faith.

A vocation to the religious state is predicated on faith and faith presumes grace. Vocation, faith, and grace are not identical but have this in common, none is experiential. Faith is predicated on things "unseen" and vocation belongs to that context.

We are familiar with the gospel texts: "You have not chosen me but I have chosen you" (Jn 15:16). "Impose not hands lightly on any man" (1 Tm 5:22). "And no man takes the honor to himself unless he is called as Aaron was" (Heb 5:4). Spiritual writers in the past may have taken these texts out of context and in so doing have created unnecessary difficulties concerning vocation. This is not simply: "I have chosen you," but works both ways, the Lord calling and the subject responding.

There was a tendency to confuse vocation with a charismatic intervention of the Holy Spirit and even the term "charism" is currently used in a loose sense. The priesthood is charismatic but a vocation to it is not the priesthood. A charism is the result of the Holy Spirit's intervention in time, its recipient being rendered capable of acts he could not possibly perform in virtue of his own powers, for example, "speaking in tongues." In this sense the priesthood is a charism, for a man could not effect transubstantiation nor forgive sins in his own person. The transformation of the person by the charismatic nature of ordination makes these actions possible.

The Notion of Consecration

The consecrated virgin, the religious in vows, too, is transformed and set apart. It is not the same transformation that takes place in baptism because the sacramental transformation that takes place in baptism is a transformation of existence. The consecration of a person in the religious life is not that but very similar. We use the word "consecration" for the Mass when speaking of the bread and wine not as being simply rendered sacred but as being transubstantiated. The consecration of a virgin in religion is analogous to that, but it is not a transubstantiation. The notion of the sacred must be distinguished from the term "holy." It means the person so consecrated, so set apart, has the efficacy of every action transformed. These actions are those of a consecrated person and they become sacred in a way in which the lay person's activity can never be sacred. This is a radical point. The clue to almost everything else about the religious life that was clarified in Vatican II lies in this notion of "consecration."

The actions of a religious brother teaching a class, a nursing sister binding a wound, a contemplative chanting the Divine Office, although physically indistinguishable from the same actions performed by a non-consecrated person, are totally different in the same way as the breathing of a baptized child differs from that of the unbaptized. The lay person teaching a class does a fine job which may, in its physical dimension of space and time, be demonstrably better than the teaching of a consecrated person. But the reality is different. What the lay person is doing has not been rendered *sacred* in the sense we are using the term. We must try to give this perspective of consecration to young religious in training, otherwise they will not be able to live by faith, and they will still ask the question: "What is the meaning of the religious life? Is there a future for it in the world today?" This type of questioning is already a failure in faith.

We must clearly understand the meaning of the term "consecration." It is not a question of one's "offering up" one's actions. For too long our spirituality has been geared to a bad theology. We have been taught that things were in themselves neutral and that we had to turn them into efficacious prayer by "getting in front of them," doing something about these actions. One had to make one's Morning Offering to make the actions of the day worshipful and meritorious. This is grounded in the philosophy that teaches there is nothing good nor bad, but our thinking makes it so. Some learn this proposition and think it is true. Equally bad is the teaching that the intention makes an act right or wrong. This is Kantian philosophy of the eighteenth and nineteenth centuries. It has invaded our spiritual thinking and formation to the point where we thought that any sort of prayer or worship must be in effect "getting behind myself" and pushing myself to do something, making various intentions in regard to what I do in order to turn it into prayer. We forget what St. Paul said: "Whether you eat or drink or whatever else you do..." (1 Cor 10:31). He was not speaking in metaphor. What he meant was that the Christian in the very act of eating or drinking was doing something appropriate to his state as a Christian, and this activity is already worshipful, just as a child in a fit of temper at the age of three is doing the only thing possible to it and is carrying out a form of worship.

In the Christian's case the act of eating is necessary and is therefore worship. In the same way, the religious' actions throughout the day are the acts of a consecrated person and are already worship. It is not a question of "getting in front of them" to change them into prayer. This could enhance their character by making them intentional prayer, but they are prayer already. Turning them into intentional prayer can heighten the person's relationship to what he is doing, but it does not turn something into prayer which is not already prayer. It is already consecrated activity.

We have lost sight also, not of the instrumental value, but of the intrinsic value of actions done by a consecrated person in grace. The principle is this: every act of a consecrated person in grace is already sacred. Our thinking has been so long conditioned by utilitarian, instrumental values that we have forgotten there are any intrinsic values. When the question is asked: "Is there a future for the religious life?" the implication is: "For what purpose is the religious life valuable as an instrument? What utilitarian purpose does it have?" Vatican II did not define it because it had any utilitarian purpose. Religious life is strictly an essential for its intrinsic value in showing forth God's glory in a special way. The actions of a consecrated person in grace show forth God's glory in a way in which nothing else can. This is the notion of the "witness" of religious. Their witnessing lies not in the utilitarian purpose of what they are doing but in the essential state of what they are. All the rest is entirely irrelevant, secondary, trivial.

We tend to get things upside-down, so we evaluate in terms of consequences. Usually this is very misleading. This is the same criterion one finds in the question asked by the disciples to Christ: "Will you at this time restore the kingdom to Israel?" (Acts 1:6). This is not the purpose of the redemption, any more than is producing more and more children capable of reading and writing the purpose of the religious life. These are good purposes but not the sole and essential purpose, the essential one being to be someone consecrated to God and thereby to have every single act of one's life transformed.

Vocation to the religious life and the priesthood are not two distinct vocations but a single continuum. There are many steps in the sacrament of holy orders, the minor orders up to and including subdiaconate being the necessary steps the candidate goes through but not part of the sacrament. Each successive step presupposes the next up to the "laying on of hands." Even the first tonsure before these steps begin is a form of the person's consecration. The cleric is already set apart "for the gospel." Since Vatican II the ministry of the Word has once more been placed in its proper context in the notion of the priesthood. Though the priesthood is primarily sacrificial, the priest's role is also salvific through the ministry of the Word. The first injunction to the apostles and through them to the priesthood is to teach: "Go teach all nations..." (Mt 28:19).

It is clear that there are not enough priests to go around and fully implement the office of preaching. Religious life is the providential solution. Vocation to the religious life forms a continuity with the priesthood. It is at one and the same time sacrificial and a sharing in the ministry of the Word. This vocation is analogous to the steps in the minor orders of ordination, part of the "setting apart for the gospel." The consecration of a brother or sister in the religious life is a sharing in the priesthood, though not in its sacramental nor charismatic dimension. The religious life is a closer sharing in the priesthood than that of the "royal priesthood" of the laity.

2. THE THEOLOGY OF VOCATION

To understand the theology of vocation we need four distinct concepts:

(1) We must distinguish the divine call itself from the processes of the human mind with regard to the divine call; the call is not something experienced. It is not a question of "Samuel, Samuel" (1 S 3:4) in the middle of the night; neither is it a "Come, follow me" (Mt 9:9) to Matthew at the money-changing table. The call, like faith, rests in the still "center of the soul," to use Abbot Marmion's phrase and in this it is comparable to the call to redemption.

(2) The experienced desire or attraction is not the divine call. The reason for this is clear since these desires and attractions can exist in those who are not called. Many wish to offer themselves; they would give anything to achieve the goal of the priesthood or the religious life, but they are not called. Not only is this experienced desire or attraction not to be identified with the divine call, but the latter may be manifested by the experience of revulsion from or refusal of a religious vocation. A feeling of revulsion from the sacrificial element of the religious vocation can in fact be the first experienced state of one who is truly called.

(3) The third factor is the "external vocation," the "juridical call" by legitimate authority. There is no vocation when this is absent. However it does not follow that its presence alone is sufficient to create a vocation. The mistake

in the past was to confuse the juridical status of being a religious with the nature of vocation itself.

(4) The fourth factor is the "fiat" of the one called. It is this factor which formalizes and clinches the vocation and without it the vocation does not exist.

What does the divine call effect if it is not experienced? It brings about a favorable will, not the consciousness of being called nor the experience of God, not even an "experience of grace," but a favorably disposed will, the individual retaining his freedom to accept or reject.

There is a vocation to the religious life and to Christian perfection, the two being distinct. The current trend in popular thinking even among religious is to confuse the two, looking upon the former as a more perfect state of the Christian's call to perfection. The vocation to Christian perfection is for all mankind just as are faith and grace. In God's Providence creation and redemption are this vocation to perfection: "This is the will of God: your sanctification" (1 Thess 4:3). The vocation to the religious life is a specification within the creation-redemption continuum. It is a further dimension of creation-redemption and is not identical with it. For this reason the vocation to the religious life, like that of the sacrificial priesthood, is for the good of others and not primarily for the person receiving the vocation.

Vocation to the religious life is a reality qualitatively different from and added to the call to Christian perfection. That is why in Canon Law the status of religious differs from that of the laity, and from lay persons who are in vows but who are not in fact consecrated religious. In Canon Law members of lay institutes are lay people, not religious. Hence it is not the taking of vows that makes the difference.

The taking of vows is a closer approximation to Christian perfection for the few who have been given this grace. But the vocation to the religious life does not lie precisely in the vows. Where, then, does it lie? It lies in the process whereby some who, on the occasion of making their vows, are publicly consecrated by the Church. This public consecration on the part of the Church sets them apart as something sacred.

With reference to religious vocation, there is much confused thinking. We know that we should expect this because the pseudo-prophets are indeed to arrive and seduce, if possible, even the elect. Part of the seduction is the contemporary teaching that the elect are to look for a criterion which would validate the nature of the religious vocation. So we hear the question: "What am I doing that a lay person could not do just as well in the world? Why am I segregated in a convent or monastery? Lay people can be just as holy as religious. Could I not go down into the slums, live with the poor and serve them that way?" The answer is: "Indeed, yes. There are many holy lay people; there is a service lay people can do just as there is a social service religious can do." The point at issue, however, is that these criteria are not those of vocation, nor are they a validation of vocation. There is no criterion outside the soul whereby one can evaluate a vocation to the religious life. Vocation is primarily the Holy Spirit's intervention predicated on faith. This means that the formal cause of vocation is the divine call.

Vocation to the religious life originates in God. This does not imply that other vocations are not divine in origin since all vocations possible for Christians are divine. But the vocation to the religious life is a divine call in a special sense in which the end-result is "union." It is predicated on union and not on service. We know that the call to the religious life is not given primarily for the sanctification of the one called but for the good of the People of God. Why, then, doesn't vocation consist in service, in teaching, or other forms of activity? We must bear in mind that the divine call is for "union" and for the good of the People of God simultaneously, and it is here that the question of "witness" arises. In what does the "witness" of religious life consist? In being the consecrated person, this unique thing to which the consecrated bears testimony, viz, to the possibility of a sacrificial life and the realization of Christian perfection. In this way, the religious belongs to the "history of salvation" for the People of God.

This means thinking not in new categories—because these are the most ancient of categories—however it does mean perhaps learning to apply unfamiliar categories in areas where we thought we knew all the answers. One of the Council's principles was that the Church was not tied to any one culture or way of life, least of all to that of the Mediterranean basin. This is the next clue for the religious life. All societies lasting through time are subject to a hardening of their "spiritual and cultural arteries." This is inevitable. All individuals living long enough jell in their thinking and it is often said that one cannot form a new idea after the age of forty. Moreover, people always tend to be praising the former generation which appears better than the present one. Regarding the religious life, the Council simply lays down the principle that it must be related to the existing culture. This is a truly revolutionary concept. It is of course, so familiar now from reading the Council documents that we don't fully appreciate just how revolutionary it is, but it is certainly much more revolutionary than the change from Latin into the vernacular in the liturgy.

All institutions created by man must be kept under constant scrutiny. The difference between the mutability of these institutions and the immutability of the divine emerges here: the radical concept is that nothing sacred or immutable has been created by man, only the divine is sacred and immutable. The religious life becomes sacred because of its relationship to the divine. All the rest is of human devising. This does not mean that we should start a big revolution, but it does mean we should re-think the very thinking that gave rise to religious life; secondly, re-thinking our own beliefs and attitudes which may be faulty in many ways; thirdly, it means relating all that is of human devising to its purpose.

First, re-thinking the very thinking that gave rise to religious life. What originated the religious state was the implementation of the evangelical counsels. The question is not whether these counsels ought to be implemented, but rather how they are best implemented? This is where human devising comes in because everytime we try to implement them, it has to be by some human device, some institution or place or behavior devised by man.

Secondly, re-thinking our own beliefs and attitudes which may be faulty in many ways. In a sense, the Church's history is one of constant, consistent, and relentless renewal. We have only to remind ourselves of some of the great renewals of the past to see how this question we have just asked is answered, namely, how best to implement the counsels? Recall St. Benedict and his renewal after the period of the hermits in the desert; St. Bernard and his renewal of the Cistercian life; St. Teresa and her renewal of the Carmelite life; St. Ignatius and his renewal of the whole structure of religion and the religious life of his time. The ways in which religious life was implemented in successive renewals were all related to the culture in which the renewal was taking place. So there is nothing new in the concept of relating this life to its cultural background. The essential point is that religious vocation, religious life, and religious institutions are all reflections of their culture.

Religious vocation and religious life reflect the culture in which they exist. The notion of culture here means a way of life, not high intellectual or aesthetic achievements. We speak of the agricultural community, a people of a nomadic culture, people of an urban culture, and we mean the kind of life these people are living. The greatest insight of Vatican II was that the structure and function of religious life must reflect the socio-political-cultural dimensions of the People of God in the world today. To clarify this, let us state another principle: every culture produces its own vocations. We recognize this with regard to the notion of a "native clergy or sisterhood." However, we do not see it in the much wider meaning of that principle, which is not a question of caste, race, nationality, but of a socio-cultural milieu, a way of life for a people. The Church, existing in various circumstances, has used the discoveries of different cultures to explain and spread the message of Christ to all nations. Its mission is to all peoples of every time and place, not being bound exclusively to any race or nation, customary way of life, recent or ancient. This last point is important in the matter of renewal, for we could add: the Church is not bound to the customary way of life of any particular institute or institution.

A vocation is a reflection of the society in which it occurs. Every society has a culture, producing its own appropriate vocations, and it follows that every culture will produce its own form of religious life. The problem for religious throughout the world is to wonder about the appropriateness of the human dimension of their life. This is the only question that is open, but it gets confused. Whether or not the evangelical counsels are to be implemented, whether the vows of chastity, poverty, and obedience are meaningful, these are not open questions. But what human devices have we created to implement these counsels? This is the question that is open.

Psychological Fitness

How does a person know whether he/she has a vocation? The discerning of vocation must lie in the area of human events and human activity, because neither grace nor vocation is experiential. The divine call takes place through human events such as fitness and acceptance on the Church's part. This "fitness" is not only a physical state of well-being but the fitness of the whole personality. This is sometimes called "psychological fitness" and it means first the absence of pathological factors in the personality. By this we mean serious disorders such as actual illness, latent morbidity, sick emotions, mental deficiency. The presence of any one of these things means that the personality so afflicted is not psychologically fit for the burdens of the religious life.

We were not particularly careful about these factors in the past because the world was not. We did not sufficiently understand the nature of these disorders and could not diagnose them adequately. It is said that if we apply the categories of psychopathology to the discerning of vocations we shall lose a great many excellent ones. Inevitably reference is made to the Curé of Ars and St. Joseph of Cupertino. If one had had psychological screening in those days, two saints would have been excluded. When we look into these cases, we understand more clearly what we mean by psychological screening. In both cases these men were not mentally defective nor lacking in intelligence. What was missing was a basic primary and secondary education. The Curé of Ars was very intelligent and this is what psychological investigation would have revealed. There were saints who seem to have been neurotic, but this does not mean that we should not try to discover neurotic or psychotic personalities as early as possible in the formation process and decide that such persons should not enter the religious life. Our role is to act as conscientiously as possible on human evidence.

The first psychological factor is negative, namely, the absence of psychopathology. The second is positive. The person having a vocation must be capable of sustaining the burdens of religious life. This obviously means that he or she has the necessary intelligence to take the kind of training required and to carry out the tasks undertaken by the community joined. It also implies an adequate understanding of and the capacity to sustain the obligations of the religious life such as chastity and obedience. Finally, this psychological fitness includes the capacity to grow into maturity as a person. The dimensions of physical and psychological suitability have to be discerned in a human way. It is helpful but not always necessary to have professional skills available because the task is sometimes difficult.

"Temporary" Vocation

Some religious are puzzled about the matter of a "temporary vocation." Is a person called to the religious state for a certain length of time? The answer is no. The term "temporary vocation" was invented to explain the fact that some individuals seem to function adequately for a time, but later on appear unable to sustain the burdens of the religious life any longer. They apply for a dispensation. The explanation given was that they were called by God for a period of a few years so that they would be better Christians upon their return to secular life. This is an error because it is not possible in the ordinary workings of Providence that the Holy Spirit would intervene temporarily in a person's life with a call to total consecration, only later to change his mind. The confusion here, one is tempted to suggest, is that between "taking vows" and "being a religious." The taking of vows does not constitute the person a religious. Rather the taking of vows is a special language through which the person expresses something and on the occasion of doing so the Church, acting in Christ's name, carries out the rite of consecration. The religious is a consecrated person and the Church carries out this consecration. As we said before, it is qualitatively different from the consecration that takes place in baptism.

In speaking then about a "temporary vocation," we are speaking about a situation which arose in the Church and which is being rectified, a situation where two things have to be kept in mind: the divine call, and the human means of discerning this call. The divine call is not experiential. It must be inferred from human evidence and it is possible for human error to intervene. People were admitted to the religious life who were thought to have a call but in fact did not. Superiors may have been mistaken in judging their fitness, or the fourth factor was missing, the "fiat" whereby one chooses this way of life forever. In the absence of this factor the vocation does not exist. God's call is not itself the vocation but simply an invitation, and we remain free to create or not create it by our own free choice or "fiat."

There is also a curious doctrine which teaches we are the passive recipients of a vocation. However, the term "vocation" is not being used properly as a noun. It is not a thing given, possessed, retained, lost. Rather it is a continuous relationship between God and the person. A person is the active contributing party to the living reality of the relationship which is the vocation we are speaking about. It is created by the first, "Yes, I come" which is the formalizing factor establishing the dialogue. The vocation continues to exist only by its being continually renewed, for it is an activity of continuous choosing. We have confused the status of "being a religious" with the vocation to become one. The status is created by the juridical procedure at the taking of the vows. This is how one enters the state. However the vocation itself must be a continuous exchange of choices—God choosing and the person responding.

The objection is raised that this way of thinking about vocation comes in conflict with the finality of the vows. Here again the problem is one of confusion between the status and the vocation. The status is final once the final vows are pronounced, unless a legitimate dispensation is obtained. The vocation itself can cease even in the consecrated person unless it is renewed. What is called a "temporary vocation" can mean either the existence of human error in judging the presence of a vocation which never existed, or else the absence of this constant renewal. This renewal is done implicitly by the observance of the rule, the prayer-life, and community love. But more and more it must become explicit, deliberate, conscious. In this it resembles faith.

As we mentioned earlier, there is confusion today between the call to Christian perfection and the religious life. We must see these calls as radically distinct. The confusion here is great, creating more problems than anything else. The religious finds it difficult to define the difference and this shakes the morale of young people. There is confusion between the concepts of renewal and mitigation of the rule, between renewal and change in the essence of the religious life. It must be quite clear that renewal, re-thinking human devices, does not mean mitigation. Rather, it is distinguishing between means and ends.

PART II: FORMATION

3. GRACE AND HUMAN PERSONALITY

There are two contrasting views of man—the naturalistic and the theological. These two views seem contradictory or mutually exclusive. Their relationship is not always understood even by those holding to the priority of the theological viewpoint. This is easy to understand when we realize that the question of man and his perfection sets us on the threshold of the most difficult problem for the human mind to study.

The naturalistic viewpoint sees no place for grace, faith, or eternal values in the scheme of things. Man is at the center of his world and his human perfecting becomes the supreme goal. The theological world-view sometimes feels threatened by this naturalistic viewpoint. The very notion of "humanism" has become a danger signal instead of being at the very core of its faith. The theological world-view appears at times to seek refuge in the supernatural, attributing to grace a causality it does not possess to solve problems on the natural plane. This is particularly true of the problem of human perfection, for the ultimate criterion has been laid down in the gospel: "What does it profit a man to gain the whole world and suffer the loss of his soul?" (Mt 16:26). Clearly, if the choice has to be made between a temporal good and the life of grace, one's line of action is clear, he must choose the life of grace. But equally clear is the fact that many temporal goods are real and intrinsic values and hence worthy objects of human striving.

In its *Constitution on the Church in the Modern World*, Vatican II echoes the words of the pagan poet: *"Humani nihil a me alienum puto,"* ("I consider nothing human to be alien to me") making it clear that it is concerned with all things human. Among the intrinsic goods of this world is the fully formed and rightly functioning human personality. The Incarnation is the source and guarantee of this. In what does human perfection consist? How should we understand its relationship to grace? Must we opt out of the world and concentrate solely on grace? Some were called to do this and some may still be called, for "In my father's house there are many mansions" (Jn 14:2).

Does Christian perfection lie in the contemplation of divine things, excluding all others as Hugh of St. Victor and others seem to have thought in medieval times? Yes and no. Yes, in the sense that our lives must be totally God-centered; no, in the sense that all are not called to leave everything and live according to the evangelical counsels. "Go, sell what you have... and follow me" (Mk 10:21) was said only to those who had ears to hear. This is not Providence's way in the world. The fact that there is a higher good, e.g., the contemplative vocation, does not lessen the value of other goods. And to say that there are other goods such as the intellectual life, creative artistic production, beauty, mental and physical health, social harmony and peace, the service of others, is in no way lessening the value of the lives of those specially chosen for a higher good. Indeed, we should remind ourselves that Pius XII, addressing superiors of contemplative orders, urged them to steep their members in the humanities and the intellectual life, for nothing good, true, and beautiful could be alien to the Christian view of the world. This same notion is stressed frequently in Vatican II.

A New Pelagianism

Our problem is that of the relationship between these different goods. Are we confronted with Pascal's dilemma: A choice between the peasant's simple faith or human nature's natural perfecting? Or are we currently being pushed into a Pelagianism, a new version of the doctrine of the perfectibility of human nature by human means alone? The former dichotomy was never truly the Christian's choice and it is clearly not so since the Council. Vatican II has stated: "It remains each man's duty to retain an understanding of the whole human person in which the values of the intellect, will, conscience, and fraternity are pre-eminent."

The perfecting of human nature seems to be the real problem when we get deeply involved in educational questions or in the psychological processes related to mental health. What is the relationship between the various natural processes of maturation, education, and the production of optimal mental functioning on the one hand, and the perfecting through grace of the Christian soul on the other? Is the former a means to the latter or vice versa? Are they unrelated, opposed? How is psychological welfare related to spiritual welfare?

Let us look at the two world-views—the naturalistic and the theological. According to the former viewpoint, everything real is observable by the senses, and man does not differ from other creatures, organic or inorganic. His perfection then lies totally in the temporal order. According to the theological viewpoint, none of these propositions will be really true. The most important real things are not visible at all, for example, God, spirit, love, grace, faith, sin, guilt. Again, man differs essentially from other creatures inasmuch as a vital part of him can escape the limitations of the space-time continuum. Consequently, his perfection cannot be achieved within the temporal order. But, and here is the crux of the problem, the theological viewpoint, accepting the reality of grace, will not lead to any new observations of phenomena not made by the naturalistic viewpoint. Nor will grace of itself cure our temporal ills: poverty, famine, war, ignorance, illness. It is our privilege to be God's instruments in doing these things.

The theological view will hold that all observed facts must be borne in mind simultaneously, not a selection among them. It will try to see the whole at the intersection of two frames of reference: the world of experience in the space-time dimension, and the transformed meaning of the whole, because man is man and God is God. The facts will not be different; grace leaves everything that can be observed exactly as it was. As Fransen expresses it: The sciences remain undisturbed by grace as long as they study observable facts in time. How then are we to comprehend man at his best in the order of nature and man perfected by grace? Is there a choice here? Must one be sacrificed for the other? What is the real meaning of St. Augustine's words: "God did not choose to save man through dialectics"?

Man alone, among all creatures, has the privilege and problem of being turned into the being he ought to be.

In the case of other living organisms a combination of the right genes and the appropriate environment are enough to ensure the realization of their goals. The genes represent the possibility of responses evoked by the environment and the latter represents the activation and satisfaction of the demands within the genetic structure.

In the case of man, he has to create the environment first and then teach the appropriate demands before they can be activated, much less satisfied. There is no automatic growth in his case towards his important goals. He must set these for himself and later choose the means of attaining them. True, he possesses many possible goals and means. Goals vary in their worthwhileness and means vary in their efficacy. But choose he must. Viewed in this way, education, formation, personality development and the processes of humanization and socialization, all are as necessary as are our genetic inheritance in the lifelong task of becoming man. Other creatures grow passively, inexorably into what they are destined to be, but man can and must choose his own humanization. The "self-realization" of the modern psychologist requires society and the means it provides for this, just as surely as it needs an appropriate, genetic inheritance. The processes of formation turning us into human beings are both a limitation and a liberation. In other words, the realization of one's full potentialities as a human being means the release of one's rational functions from the dominance of the non- or pre-rational factors, while at the same time the possible range of behavior is limited by the curbs of society.

Even when the rational functions have been released, even where the necessary social curbs are operative, there still remains the task of building the mature person and perfecting him through grace. Obviously in considering the perfection of this human personality we need the co-operation or better the cross-fertilization of the two approaches to man—the naturalistic and the theological. When we have done this, we shall see that they are not distinct processes but form a consistent whole. Each stands in need of the other. The empirical scientist needs the moral philosopher and the theologian to set the goal, assess values, give direction. And these two require all the help they can get from psychology, education, and the allied sciences. Each problem of goal, conduct, or value has two different sets of coordinates, two frames of reference: man as an individual of the species in the physical world, and man as transcending the whole physical world.

The problem is not a choice between two possibilities, one temporal and the other supernatural, but rather that man is both of these simultaneously. This is precisely the problem of his perfection: he must achieve the highest level of functioning possible in the natural order and become something wholly other in the supernatural order. Just as the naturalistic viewpoint has blurred this distinction by assimilating the supernatural to the natural order, so too have theologians obscured the distinction by assimilating the natural to the supernatural. The scientist will not be able to observe grace in the world or in the person. The behavior of a man talking with the "tongues of angels" and "having charity" will not possess an observable dimension differing from the man lacking these things. On the other hand, the theologian must avoid the error of looking upon grace as something added to the act which remains substantially as it was before. Rather, the whole reality of the act is changed but not observable. Grace leaves everything as it was, yet changes everything utterly. The change, however, is in the innermost nature or being of things.

Let me illustrate this by recalling two familiar facts: the intelligence of a mentally retarded child is not improved even after the child is baptized. The normal child must be turned into a man through his parents and teachers. Similarly, a mentally-ill patient is cured of his illness by natural means and not by grace. Only on being cured does he become capable of a free worship of God.

Grace and Natural Perfection

The relationship between grace and natural perfection may be expressed thus: the natural act is the "herald making straight the path" (Mk 1:3) for the flowing of grace. Grace, as we said, will not produce any natural improvement in us; it will not, for instance, increase a dull child's intelligence. Neither will it relieve anxiety or cure natural ills. And yet, it is the most important reality in our life.

How are we to understand the Church's pre-occupation with the perfecting of personality in the natural order? Should she not concentrate on the supernatural order? Why should she be occupied with teaching secular subjects since "one thing is necessary" (Lk 10:42)? "Seek first the kingdom of God and his justice and all things will be added to you" (Mt 6:33). Should the Church avoid all things and concentrate solely upon the "pearl of great price"? The answer is no. Our task is the "restoration of all things in Christ." While it is true that the natural processes are not our full perfecting, yet our perfecting in the order of grace is unlikely in their absence in the ordinary workings of divine Providence. St. Paul declares: "How can they believe unless they hear, and how can they hear unless someone preaches to them?" (Rm 10:14). This shows the dependence of salvation on natural means. Our role as teachers is that of secondary causes, helping others achieve the goal of redemption. Supposing the redemption was accepted by mankind, would our goal as teachers be different? No. There would still be the necessity of educating the young, forming them in Christ, healing their ills, caring for their defects. The task would be easier but we would still have to do it.

To reach a goal we must know what it is. We have a fairly clear idea of our supernatural goal, but frequently we are vague about our goal of becoming mature persons. What is the plan for us here on earth? What kind of creature did God intend us to be? Surely he intended us to be formed in the image of his Son. It appears as though the goal of the believing, morally good Christian and that of the fully mature person on the natural plane were in conflict. This is because of the confusion about the relationship of grace to nature.

It is not the role of grace to produce the fully mature person. This is our goal as teachers. We usually have clear ideas concerning the moral qualities of the mature person, however we are not clear about his personality dimensions. Indeed, we seem to fear the mature adult as though he somehow came in conflict with the Christian virtues of docility, humility, love, and obedience. We seem to have forgotten some of the other virtues such as magnanimity, the virtue of greatness of soul inclining one to accomplish great things for the sake of God.

Unfortunately, too, we have looked upon rationality and maturity as somehow opposed to faith instead of seeing them as its prerequisites in the ordinary ways of Providence.

Some of our problems and anxieties on the intellectual level are due to this mistaken notion. Men of good will sometimes seem to misunderstand the perfectly good, healthy, desirable seeking of the highest functioning of rationality and maturity, equating them with "rationalism." Our maturity as persons does not conflict with our goal as Christians. Properly understood, the former is a means to the latter. To be mature means to be mentally healthy and to remain immature, unformed as a person, means to fall short of the mark set for us in our creation by God.

There are some who think the "little way" of St. Therese of Lisieux or our Lord's injunction to "become as little children" somehow mean that there is virtue in being immature. The little way is in fact for very mature persons and "becoming little children" has nothing to do with childishness but with child-likeness which is being single-minded, having clarity of vision, purity of heart, and real love.

It is not too difficult to recognize the mature person. He meets with ease the normal demands of his surroundings. He has reached the stage of emotional control, accepting the uniqueness and incommunicability of being a person. Responsibility is the norm of his life, not a threat to his security. He appreciates some measure of stability in his life but he can adapt readily to a changing environment. His ambitions are realistic and within the scope of practical realization. The mature person does not indulge in fantasies and romantic dreams to escape life's real problems. In possession of a realization of his weaknesses, he is also acquainted with his strong points. He can be helpful to others while accepting help from others. His faith, personal beliefs, and values are a source of strength to him and his patterns of behavior are consistent with these. The mature person is open to receive others, accepting and loving them as they are. He never looks upon another person as a thing or symbol. He accepts the other without judgment, evaluation, or prejudice which is perfect love. Psychological maturity can be dated with fair accuracy from the time two significant things occur: emotional control is established, one realizes his uniqueness and aloneness before God. Both factors require self-knowledge. Without this we cannot hope for emotional control, nor can we separate our judgments from our feelings. We must make ourselves what we ought to be, however we cannot achieve this if we are ignorant of what we ought to be.

Intellectual maturity is an indispensable component of maturity proper. For a long time we have not admitted explicitly that we are specified in our nature by our intellect. In extolling the cultivation of the intellect we are praising the most essential component of human perfection on the natural plane. Intellectual attainment, therefore, should never be feared as a danger to faith or an occasion of pride. The real danger lies in not pursuing the intellectual life sufficiently. There is no virtue in a lack of knowledge, and we should emphasize more the fact that knowledge is a virtue proper to the intellect. God is glorified by the very existence of knowledge in a Christian soul. We have forgotten this intrinsic knowledge, adopting a purely instrumental attitude towards it. Knowledge is not valuable only because it can be put to use but because God is knowledge as well as love. His knowledge is prior to his love as the intellect holds primacy over the will. He could have endowed us with infused knowledge but has not done so. We must achieve it through natural means. Since the Reformation the Christian mind has suffered from a certain "malaise" regarding the intellect. Each advance in science has been represented by its discoverers as a threat to the faith and has been looked upon as such by believers. We have only to recall the discoveries in physics, chemistry, biology, and most recently in psychology. Each in turn put forward an answer to the faith and each was encountered as a danger.

The real danger for the Christian world lies in our failure to appreciate the truth-content, the intrinsic value, and the glory of God manifested in these studies. All that exists is given to us to know. The error of some well-intentioned men at the time of the Reformation was that they did not see the cultural revolution taking place before their eyes. Many ills of the past few centuries are due to the failure to understand that it was and is part of the Church's mission to develop human values, the greatest of which is the development of the human personality. As the cultural level rises, so must the Church rise always higher in proportion. Within the Church, the level of discovery, research, creative achievement ought to outdistance those of the purely naturalistic culture. This is so, not for any utilitarian value, neurotic and competitive motives, nor even primarily for mission motives, but for their intrinsic values.

There are two points to be stressed in this connection. First, because the redemption has taken place, being a Christian should be looked upon as the only legitimate way open to us now to be human beings. Instead of seeing the Church as a society placed alongside other societies, to which one belongs as one might to any humanly devised society, we must begin to view it as a way for human beings to realize their future stature as persons. "The restoration of all things in Christ" extends to the outermost limits of human achievement.

Secondly, Vatican II has made abundantly clear our obligations to achieve a deep and productive awareness of the various disciplines of knowledge, the range of the arts, the richness of different cultures. We are no longer entitled, if indeed we ever were, to opt out of human values and secular pursuits as these are part of our perfecting as human beings. To call them "secular" is wrong when it is intended to contrast them with "Christian."

Confidence in Man

It is thought there is something contradictory in the notion of the Christian's seeking such values. It seems as though he is seeking his perfection here below or attaching too much value to the temporal order. The objection runs: If we are truly consistent, would we not strive exclusively for the next life? As we already said, whenever a temporal value or good endangers eternal life, the answer is clear: we cannot sacrifice the latter for the former. This is not the point at issue. The question is: How are we to conceive our perfection as creatures in time in relation to our eternal destiny? How do we understand the Christian's relationship to temporal values, including those of personality and intellectual development? The answer lies in the theology of the Incarnation. As the second Person of the Trinity became man, so also must we become man.

For many centuries we have thought in terms of making men Christians. Should we not begin to think of making Christians men? This means the removal of the barriers, namely, poverty, fear, aggression, and ignorance; enabling our fellowman to make the right choices through education and cultural formation. This is the *raison d'être* of our great educational foundations. This is why the Church is involved in education. The vote of confidence in man and in God entailed in the Council document on Religious Liberty should have healthy repercussions in the Church's intellectual life. The reason is that it has enhanced rather than diminished our responsibilities for our own perfecting. The degree of responsibility is the measure of our human stature.

Formation in responsibility means formation in self-control. This in turn means formation of the person so that consciousness, the rational principle or ego, is capable of initiating, directing, channeling, or permitting the kind of behavior appropriate to a person. There is nothing here of weakness, immaturity, passivity, or unrealistic fantasy. Yet one suspects that sometimes by contrasting these traits with the more formidable ones of strong-mindedness, goal-choosing, leadership-exercising, autonomy, we may have arrived at thinking of the former as virtues and the latter as dangers.

Is this not a failure in faith? If God created us to be this kind of creature, responsible for our eternal destiny, why is it so difficult to concede this status to ourselves? The answer is found in a perfectly intelligible anxiety. Curiously, it is due to our fellowman that we find it so difficult to respect his unique autonomy, just as a mother finds it hard to concede the fact that her child has grown up. Formation for responsibility and, through this, for perfection is the lifelong task of releasing the rational functions of man from the distorting effects of the irrational so that he may achieve a healthy harmony.

Responsibility is the natural underpinning of grace. Let us turn to the relationship of grace to our perfection. Some have contended that the soul's welfare and that of the psyche are one, thereby implying that the practice of religion, the increase of grace in the soul, is also our natural perfecting. This is curiously latent in Jung's theories and has been accepted by some of our theologians. But this is erroneous, taking as it does the reality of grace into the space-time dimension. Thus grace is no longer grace. It also forgets our role in formation. More particularly, it equates sin with mental illness, mental well-being with grace. Instead of defending the theological world-view, intended by its advocates, it becomes a version of the naturalistic viewpoint.

There is no reason why the mentally defective child should not see God in eternity, or why the neurotic should not grow ever closer to him through grace, or why there should not be an ever-increasing growth of grace in the psychotic's soul. This does not imply that we should exert no effort to restore mental health to these weaker brethren. It is clear that, properly used, mental health will be an even more fruitful soil for growth in grace because the human dimension of the human act will be enhanced.

Considering now our meaning of the mentally healthy adult, we shall recognize that we do not mean a person free from pathology of one kind or another. We mean the fully developed person who has realized his potentialities and is functioning at the upper threshold of his possibilities. None of us is as far advanced as that since there is still room for advance up the scale of maturity in each of us.

The natural processes of education, personality formation, perfecting human values, are seen in the Christo-centric view of the universe as the mission of the Baptist. Just as

John was not the "Christ" but the "herald" who made the "rough ways smooth and the crooked paths straight," so the psychological skills and the educative processes producing the mature person are the opening of the highways of grace.

The theology of grace and the problem of personality and perfection may be summed up as follows: Our becoming man is conditional on the processes of education and formation in our human society. Our being redeemed is conditional on our being men. The natural processes are not what brings about our perfecting as this would spell Pelagianism. However, without these processes our salvation would not be assured, for these are God's ways of perfecting us.

Revelation and redemption are direct, divine actions. What we are concerned with is our involvement as real but secondary causes in the working out of the redemption. The new discoveries of human knowledge, the better understanding of how to bring about the good society, deeper compassion, these are all results of Christ's saving acts, while at the same time they are the Baptist's work: "making smooth the rough ways and making straight the paths" for the advent of Christ's grace. It is frequently forgotten that this takes place for most men through ordinary daily living.

This is the real mission of salvation, not that the ordinary chores of living are God's grace but the passage of this grace is through ordinary channels. Just as God has transformed the reality of bread and wine, water, oil, etc., so too he can transform the reality of society and of our own actions within society, not in a miraculous way, not by producing any new, discernible dimension, but by the most radical change of all, namely, a change of the substance and being of our lives, our society, ourselves. That is where grace resides and that is what it effects, but we must perform the acts. Then, because we are transformed by the presence of grace, our actions are transformed in their source and essence. By a theological cybernetic principle of feedback we are then transformed in turn by our acts, not in any discernible dimension but in our being. Thus this change of ourselves in turn reacts on our activity and there commences the eternal circle of person and act. This is where prayer resides, for all such acts show forth God's glory and are then the highest form of prayer.

4. ACTS AND MOTIVES

Psychology and the understanding of the human act are relevant at all levels to our understanding of human behavior. The more we understand human behavior, the better position we are in to facilitate the operation of grace in ourselves and to form the young under our care. The human act and its underlying motives will, therefore, be the subject of this present chapter.

All of us perform many types of acts but it seems they fall into one of two categories—indeliberate acts because we are organisms, deliberate acts because we are persons. The former include basic metabolism, bodily reflexes, and unconscious acts; the latter, those acts that are free and responsible, meritorious or culpable.

Behavior

We must distinguish between two kinds of behavior—learned and unlearned. What the organism does that is merely dependent on maturation is unlearned behavior and this may be termed emergent patterns of behavior. These things are genetically determined in the sense that the genes govern both the emergence and the behavior patterns emerging. All such activity belongs to the indeliberate category. In other words, they are actions of an organism as an organism, not of a person as a person.

The relation of person to act is that of source to consequence or effect. There is a reciprocal relationship here: the person performs the acts and the acts form the personality. This is what is meant by the existentialist formula: "existence precedes essence." This is misleading when read in classic metaphysical terms, but in psychological terms it means that the child exists first and what he becomes depends on what he does. The existential formula uses the notions of "essence" and "existence" in a broad sense. Our personality is formed by our acts but these are the result of the kind of person we are.

In the child's case some actions proceed directly from internal, felt states, for example, hunger, fear, anger. When the child comes into existence there is almost no "self" present. However, there is a very rudimentary distinction in the child's first conscious act between "self" and "otherness," between the experience of self and things. Later the "self" develops. An impulse, urge, desire, or emotion wells up and issues in action; for example, the child feels hungry and cries, feels warmth and affection and responds with a smile. This is a direct effect in behavior of a cause in the psyche.

The same impulse later on will well up and have to be processed by consciousness, being either inhibited or allowed to issue in action. Control, therefore, depends on this ego or self. In the adult, both these processes remain, the possibility of one's actions issuing directly from a deep, psychological cause on the one hand, and the possibility of its being processed by consciousness on the other. The human act, therefore, is the act processed by consciousness. It is important to add intellect and will as being the formalities of the "human act" whereas acts that are not or could not be processed by consciousness remain indeliberate.

The child's behavior is essentially the result of the internal processes not processed by consciousness; they do not pass through the ego or self. The adult's behavior is essentially defined as acts processed through the ego or self. Another point: there is literally no innate knowledge on the child's part as to how to control behavior. There are certain built-in controls; for example, an action begins to emerge and the child discovers early that this will be met by pain, so pain operates to inhibit this piece of behavior. This is primitive control, not innate control. It is learned in response to the consequences of the act. Even such elementary reflexes as the control of the excretory processes have to be learned. Initially, these are fairly random pieces of behavior but very early the child begins to acquire cerebral control over them. These controls are the result of a learning process. The unlearned behavior emerges and the learning processes are grafted onto them.

This is the beginning of the conversion of the organism, a person, into a human being with a "personality." The child is born human, but all through its life it has to pass through the humanizing process which turns him into what he ought to be. All other organisms grow passively. Given an environment and the right genes they develop into what they are supposed to be. The human being has to learn to control this process by growing into what he ought to be. We call this "humanizing." Left to himself the child will be a human being in an elementary sense but never what he should become. Humanizing is the process of grafting learned patterns of behavior onto the basic unlearned patterns.

The factors producing behavior in the child still remain within the adult and are capable of producing consequences without passing through consciousness. For example, fear can produce a sinking feeling in the stomach, nausea, and fainting or unconsciousness in extreme cases. Joy can bring laughter, sorrow, tears. This is the case of efficient causality of a psychical event producing an effect in the form of overt behavior. Other processes can have similar effects; for example, the thought of scraping a piece of chalk on a blackboard produces that horrible sound in your mind and you get a tightening sensation of the jaw. This is an example of efficient causality of imagery producing behavior, and this is where the indeliberate act can be seen at the adult level. "Psychical events," events in the psyche, can and do produce their own consequences without the intervention of the will's control. Emotions and images do that.

There are other examples. Suppose you form an image of yourself standing on thin ice, about to start skating. You could first form a visual image. Then try to form an image of the movement of actually starting to skate. As you continue to form the image you find little muscular changes beginning to occur. This again is the psyche at work. In one terminology the imagery is producing muscular consequences; in another, much more philosophically correct, one psychological process is giving rise to another. There is an efficient causality between these psycho-physical events. This is not identical with efficient causality between material things but it is of the same order. This kind of causality is purposive without our choosing its purpose. We are not acting for a purpose. These are the actions of a person, but not insofar as one is a person. In the case of one listening to chalk scraping along the blackboard, there is a tightening of the jaw. This tightening does not occur because one is a person but an organism. The organism is subject to the laws of matter. Here we have another level of the things an organism does: it behaves (insofar as it is material) subject to the laws of matter from which there is no exemption. There is no special physics or chemistry that applies to organisms but not to the rest of matter; nor are there any laws of matter which will not apply to the organism because we exist in a space-time continuum. The important thing is, of course, we are not exclusively governed by this sort of law.

Whatever the organism does *qua* organism is called behavior; what it does formally as a person is conduct. Behavior becomes a genus, that is, behavior is what the organism does and conduct is a species of that genus. Conduct is specific to man and is responsible behavior.

The Notion of Conduct

The notion of conduct means the responsible, free act. Freedom is one of the great problems here. What is a free act? It is exactly in the same category as conduct or the acts of a person *qua* person. The free act is not an uncaused act. This is important, for when we begin to explain human acts, people begin to think we are denying freedom or responsibility. For example, a teenager is arraigned before the courts charged with malicious damage of public property. We could say, this youth did not enjoy the advantages of a stable home, an education, was out in the streets from the age of eleven, was emotionally disturbed, and has an I.Q. of 95. All these factors help us understand why he did what he did. Therefore he is not responsible? Not necessarily. Suppose another case—an adult of thirty. He has a good education, a good job, but now he is about to leave his wife. He is an inveterate gambler and is presently before the court for a piece of fraud. We could say, this man's home environment is unhappy; his wife never loved him; and perhaps they found traces of a schizoid personality in him. All this aids us in understanding why he is leaving his wife and why he gambled. While it helps us understand why, it does not necessarily involve the further conclusion: therefore, he is not responsible. Being able to understand the reason for an action is not the same as exonerating or exculpating one. It may be an important factor in forgiving, but forgiving is predicated on the fact that one is guilty.

The "free act" seems to suggest something which is totally devoid of determining factors. As a matter of fact, the most free of free acts is subject to tremendous determining factors. This is not at all the same as "determinism." Determining factors are those conducive to bringing about a particular act, but they don't bring it about since it is the person who does so. Nothing we do is free in the sense of having no determining factors. The notion of a human act occurring in an uncaused vacuum is a metaphysical impossibility. It would not be true to say that the difference between behavior and conduct is only one of degree. Behavior, when it is not conduct, is totally determined by factors other than the formality of one's being a person. The free act is largely subject to determining factors, but the truth is it would not come about were it not for the fact that I as a person do it.

The free act is not uncaused. What are its causes? As we mentioned earlier, some of them will be unlearned factors; some, learned, superimposed on these. The final cause will be "myself," the person, doing the act. Secondly, a free act is not unintelligible and it could not be. Whatever is real is intelligible, so the free act will be to some extent intelligible. Saying that it is intelligible and showing how does not derogate from its status of being a free act. Thirdly, the free act is not motiveless. When I indicate the motives, I am not derogating from its status as being free. You cannot have a free act which is unmotivated. Unfortunately, motive has been identified in the thinking of most of us with "purpose." We ask, why did he go to the University? Because he wanted to obtain a degree. Purpose is the motive. Why did he buy a car? Because he wanted to drive to the country or to work. We state a purpose and this is an important motive, but a motive is anything contributing in any way to the production of an act.

So in addition to purpose or final cause motives can be in any of the other categories of cause: formal, material, efficient, or final. Listing the four causes is not the same as saying, "Therefore, the act is not free." We could put this in a still more extreme form and say, you could not have an act unrelated to these causes. Efficient cause, in this case, means an event in the psyche which, other things being equal and if there is no impeding factor, will issue in an act. This is what takes place in the case of a child or adult when sudden pain issues in the act of crying, "Ouch." This is an efficient causality sequence.

The material cause, the matter going to make up the act, is the living physiology of the organism, the behavioral dimension which is turned into conduct by the formality of its being my chosen act. A reflex process, therefore, can be the result of an instinctual urge or impulse; it can also be a determined process by my making it my own by giving it a sort of formality. I become responsible for the act. We need four kinds of concepts here: the human act resulting from efficient, final, formal, and material causality, all operating simultaneously. The human act is not uncaused; it is not unintelligible; and it is not motiveless. This last aspect must be emphasized because there are those who get the idea that if they can find a motive the act is therefore vitiated as though it were not free.

It is useful to list some of the components of the human act. First, it is the act of the person. One should not get the idea that within the person one single faculty, the intellect, withdraws on its own and does its own thinking. Nor should one get the notion that the will is operating in a vacuum as a mechanism in its own right. The person acts on two levels: the conscious and the deeply unconscious. At the first level, the intellect judges something to be good and the will elicits the act; beneath the surface there is a great deal of unconscious, acquired, intellectual content operating at the same time. In other words, we do not mobilize all our intellectual knowledge in a moment and make a judgment. On the contrary, the knowledge once received remains with us dynamically as a habit or habitual knowledge in St. Thomas' terminology. As a habit it is a disposition to act. Our conscious knowledge may be minimal at any given moment, but the unconscious background may be enormous, affecting the act. On the other hand, unconscious, habitual knowledge may be minimal.

Take the vandal youth again. Perhaps he lacks the knowledge we have of right or wrong, human conduct, society, reward and punishment, mechanisms, policemen, courts, decent human relationships. His conscious knowledge may be simply: "Here I am in a public park and there is a seat and it would be good to smash it up." As far as we are concerned, all that background of acquired knowledge operates as a determinant of behavior and a blocking mechanism. When we are faced with choice: "Will I do it?" "Yes, I will," this is only a small part of the act because all the acquired habits of choosing of which we are not conscious are operating to facilitate or block the operation. This is why virtue and vice are habits or better still, this is why habitual acts can and do remain culpable or meritorious. People sometimes get the idea that it is better to operate the "slow dead heave of the will," pulling against one's inclinations than to carry out an act facilitated by acquired virtue. This is one of the great mistakes of many. In other words, it is argued that it is no great credit to sisters that they are good because they have been for twenty years processed into that and it is second-nature to them. It is only because acquired habits remain as acquired determinants that the virtuous act becomes meritorious and remains at a higher level than the individual "slow heave of the will" struggling against adverse circumstances. It is the person acting and that person's quality which determines the act, just as the act forms the personality.

Memory and Imagination

The memory operates at the conscious level too. The child, for example, may begin to recollect that he was told not to pull his sister's hair, a reasonable bit of recollection. There is, however, a mass of memories in the deep unconscious which are even more important, for example, the recollection of acts rewarded or punished, of affection won or lost, of pain experienced as a result of certain acts and pleasure as a result of others. All this is operating but not in the conscious mind.

The imagination in the sense of the capacity to form

images will also be operative. The imagination forms an image; it may be an attractive one and this operates as a final cause or purpose, or it may be an image operating as an efficient cause as in the case of trying to form an image of yourself skating on thin ice. There will be a mass of imagery operating as a determinant of behavior in the child's mind.

The purpose of education in the widest sense is to form the whole person through all these factors so that they may operate as continuing determinants. There is no good in thinking of education as the momentary repetition of phrases like: "Two plus two are four." It is education only if it sinks into the personality and continues to operate as a determinant of behavior. This is what humanization means: the potentially human being is turned into the being he ought to be by formation.

Needs, instincts, impulses are also sometimes felt at a conscious level, for example, the need for food. There can be an instinctive process, the child instinctively seeking the mother's affection or at a later level the instinctive movement of boys and girls to seek each other's company. This is experienced at a conscious level, but is operating, too, at the unconscious level and is operating in all of us.

The human act is not the act of the intellect and the will in a vacuum. The formality of the act derives from these two; however, it is the whole person who is acting. So in the human act there are discernible effects from all these factors, even at the uppermost level of the most purified intentions in the spiritual life. It is not surprising to find in an act of the highest endeavor some elements of gratification at a very organic level. This is what Nuttin means when he says: "Human motivation is never wholly spiritual or wholly rational." It could not be because we are not wholly spiritual or rational; we are the living organism.

All these things are contributory but do not necessarily operate all the time. One could conceive a situation where instinct perhaps is dormant or memory is not operative; however, in general most of them operate most of the time. This is why intellectual activity can be so tiring. If it could operate in a vacuum, then it could go on interminably.

Motivation

Human acts have six different dimensions. The conscious dimension which is obviously the most important, immediate, relevant, in terms of theology and the religious life and life experiences. At the conscious level an act may be motivated by the love of God, but at the unconscious level there may be some deep gratification involved at the level of instinctual life. For example, a preacher may love to thunder about sexual behavior. Consciously, he is motivated by a desire for his parishioners' welfare and may really be concerned about this. With a little probing, however, one might show that there is tremendous gratification at the unconscious level. He is handling his libido, but in this indirect, unhealthy way of denunciation. An ascetic carrying out some very desirable procedure may find gratification at a much deeper level. This is a danger in the physical dimensions of asceticism, the discipline, for example. The conscious motivation may certainly be reparation, mortification, self-control. Yet one may find at a deeper level in the deep unconscious a masochistic satisfaction. This does not negate the value of the consciously motivated act.

A great deal of literature seems to suggest that to reveal the deep unconscious motivation of a human act is somehow to negate its value. This is not so. One could not have a human act that did not have some of these unconscious motivations. It is the conscious act, the act processed through self, the ego, which is formally the human act. We may not be aware of all our motivations; however, if we are choosing this act for certain motivations that we are aware of then we are responsible. If these motivations are good, the act is good and vice versa. It is the conscious determinant that specifies the act, not the possibility of discovering its unconscious dimensions.

In addition to the conscious and the unconscious we have two other kinds of motivation: the acknowledged and the unacknowledged. These do not coincide with the conscious or the unconscious dimensions. One may have a conscious motive which is not currently being acknowledged. One may be aware of a kind of gratification sought in a particular relationship or activity and yet not acknowledge that it is there. This comes up very often in the behavior of young religious who may be conscious of the need for closer interpersonal relations and set up special friendships. They may not be aware, in fact by definition they could not be aware, of the deep unconscious motivation which may underlie that sort of relationship. Later on, they may acknowledge some dimensions of this relationship but not acknowledge others. The acknowledged motivation here is based on something sound which is "love one another." The unacknowledged motivation (which may not be entirely unconscious) is a need for felt affection. Felt affection is not at all the same sort of thing as the "I-thou" relationship of interpersonal identification and love. The unacknowledged need for consciously felt affection is a very dangerous dimension of the human act in that sort of society.

There are two other kinds of motivation—habitual and interpretative. An act may be carried out because of acquired dimensions in the deep unconscious which we call habits. In this way the act may be carried out without my here and now consciously eliciting it or consciously choosing its purpose, but this does not negate the human act. The acquired habit of behavior operates and the act remains meritorious.

The interpretative dimension is an entirely different matter and is not our concern at the present moment. It is the possibility of a motive operating of which I was never conscious at all, not one which was merely there because of the nature of the act I have elicited.

The human act is free but not uncaused. There is a dimension here of the human act which has not been looked into sufficiently. It is the distinction between cause and condition of the act. The causes of an act can be many: unlearned impulses of the organism, learned controls at the infantile level, conscious, unconscious, unacknowledged purposes. The formality of its being "I" doing it, plus all these things are all part of the cause of the act.

Some acts have a further dimension of being blocked or inhibited which is a different matter. In the moral order there are here and now operating in normal, mature adults tremendous blocking mechanisms, inhibiting factors, factors making it impossible for us to carry out certain acts. It is no credit to us that we do not carry them out. This is part of what is meant by: "When you have done all these things, say, we are unprofitable servants" (Lk 17:10). It is also part of the *gratia praeveniens* of theologians, preventing grace which goes before and eliminates. But it is even more than that; it is the fact of social pressures. Some of these operate by our having accepted and assimilated them with the result that they are now determinants at a very deep level of our personality. Shame is one of these determinants. It is not the same as guilt but its effects can be similar. It is a control-mechanism and society imposes these at very deep levels. They are very effective. For example, a child born in the slums, of very unstable parents, lacking in education, will be more likely to carry out certain kinds of acts that a more privileged child would not. What has happened is that conditions that ought to be there are not there; social determinants which ought to have been built into the personality are missing. Responsibility is, therefore, diminished accordingly, but we ourselves are responsible for the fact that these determinants are missing. That is why we share the guilt of the underprivileged, but we do not share the guilt of the big-time swindler who has had all the privileges and has made a bad choice.

More to the point perhaps is the relationship of the human act to predictable, statistical events. We know that something like twenty-six murders a day will take place in the U.S.A., and that something like thirteen suicides a week take place in Berlin. The question is, how are we to understand causality in regard to this sort of event? The answer again is to be found in these privations. Social factors are missing that ought to be there. Suicide is related to social isolation. It is not that being alone produces suicide, for being alone is not a cause and the absence of other people cannot be the reason why people commit suicide. Social isolation is a condition in which processes can emerge. In most of us they are blocked by social pressures. The same thing happens in smaller ways in the group. In a group of novices social pressures ensure that certain kinds of behavior take place.

There are many kinds of acts of which we are physically capable, but we will not perform these acts. It is no credit to us that we do not perform them. The fact is we could not do them, they are psychologically impossible. Yet there are social groups where they are not only psychologically possible but also predictable.

"Condition" can easily be mistaken for cause. There are conditions which permit certain acts to occur. Social dimensions, social factors, are among these permissive conditions.

The observable dimension of behavior is another important factor. This means behavior as seen from the outside. It is very easy to parallel different pieces of observable behavior as seen in the factors they have in common, however one must always be alive to the fact that the observable behavior is no guarantee of the internal processes that bring it about. To identify observable behavior with its internal processes is to commit the fallacy of psychomechanistic parallelism, the mistake of thinking that because pieces of behavior are similar, therefore the causation behind them is similar. This is important in the question of neuroses and scruples; the same piece of behavior will be discerned in two different people, repetitive, compulsive preoccupation with guilt. One individual may be mentally ill; the other may be going through the spiritual trial of scruples. The differences will lie in the psychical processes behind the discernible dimensions.

Psychology, therefore, and the understanding of the human act are, as we have seen, highly relevant at all levels to our understanding of human behavior. The more we understand human behavior, the better position we are in to facilitate the operation of grace. It is often thought that we would do better if we did not know all these things, especially if we paid no attention to deep unconscious motivations and all that sort of thing. But studying such matters could be compared to the role of the forerunner of the Messiah. It is not itself grace, it is not itself supernatural. It is almost trite to say it involves any concept other than human nature in its functioning. Just as St. John the Baptist had to go before and make straight the paths, smooth the ways, in the same way the more we can understand these processes, the easier it will be to facilitate the operation of grace in ourselves and to form the young under our care.

5. PHASES OF DEVELOPMENT

Before we can say much about the development or formation of the religious consecrated to God by public vows, we must first say something about the complex problem of personality and its development. We have labored for some time under a number of misunderstandings regarding personality. Personality in the philosophical sense is not what we are concerned with here. In this sense we are all equally persons, and we were persons from the moment of conception, from the moment of the infusion of the created soul. The newly conceived infant and the fully mature person are equally persons. No human being can be more a person than any other.

Personality Differences

In the psychological sense, however, it is quite obvious that no two persons have the same personality. That is what makes the difference between the philosophical use wherein all are equally persons on the one hand, and the obvious psychological fact on the other which is that the person sitting beside you is different from you in every conceivable way. The difference is this—as the philosopher uses the term "person" he refers to the reality of your nature, and as the psychologist uses the term "personality" he refers to the quality of being "you," not just to the fact that you are, but to the quality of being "you" and not the person beside you. To the philosopher's question, "Where does personality come from?" we can answer: "It comes from the act of creation, from God himself." To the same question in the psychological sense ("Where does personality come from?" "What makes you different from the person beside you?"), we have to say: "We are the source of that. It is you and I and all other human beings, our parents, our grandparents, the structure of society, the difference of schools, and the problems we had—all that makes you 'you' and me 'me.'"

What makes you different from the person beside you? Briefly, a combination of your heredity and your environment. In more technical terms you began to be as a set of chromosomes and genes; the genes were the determinants that you now have blue eyes, brown hair, bones of a particular structure, a special kind of nervous system, and a particular kind of cerebral cortex. The genes, the bearers of heredity, produce the determinable, organic, visible factors of "you."

We do not grow passively from a set of genes into the fully developed person. We have to add to the genes the other factor which is environment or life-history. The second set of factors that make you "you" are your life-history in the most meticulous details. What makes you different from the person beside you is the combination of genes with which you started out in life and every single subsequent event throughout your life. Obviously the genes will have a part to play, determining the type of nervous system and endocrine glandular system you have. All this means is that you can feel emotions, experience hunger, impulses, and instinctive movements. Some people feel emotion very intensely, others, in a mild, placid way. Some feel the sexual urge in a powerful way, others, in a mild way. These are the genetic differences. We call that our temperament. Your temperament is primarily a "given" with which you commence life. Temperament is the more or less predictable, abiding set of emotional inclinations which are yours and not those of the person beside you. However, there are three terms which must be kept distinct, namely, temperament, personality, and character.

The child comes into the world with a genetic endowment which ensures that he will cry and scream in anger, protest when frustrated, get hungry and tired. All this is a matter of temperament. The mother knows in the case of her first-born child that he is very explosive and warm-hearted; she knows that her second child is withdrawn, less demonstrative. She is recognizing here temperamental differences, but she will inaccurately use words like "character" and "personality" to express what she observes about each child. She will say: "It is extraordinary how different my two children are in their personalities." Actually, she is speaking about their temperaments because as yet they have no personalities.

Personality in the psychological sense begins to be constructed as soon as the child starts to do something about his emotions. When he realizes, for instance, that he cannot have the out-pouring of affection from his mother twenty-four hours a day, as soon as he begins to realize that his screaming is not always going to succeed in manipulating adult behavior, then personality begins to emerge. In other words, personality is the beginning of or begins with the formation of emotional life. From the very moment of the child's first conscious experience his personality is being formed.

The Notion of Character

Character refers to the moral quality of being "you." We do not talk about a good or bad temperament. We can speak of a volatile or placid, likable or unlikable, pleasant or unpleasant temperament, but never about a good or bad one, for it is neither morally good or bad. Character, on the other hand, is always either morally good or bad. It is a much later development than either temperament or personality. It can be defined as the acquired set of abiding moral inclinations within the personality which lead to a more or less predictable set of behavior patterns. If a child is consistently seeking ways to control his emotional life and implement the various regulations of the moral law, then we say his character is good. Character will not be formed until well on into the upper teens, perhaps not even until the middle twenties or thirties.

These three factors interact all the time, but they must be kept distinct. The qualities of personality are not virtues, those of character are. We all have mistaken personality qualities for those of character, for example, we confuse affection with charity. It is easy to feel affectionate towards someone because that is temperament at work; however, it is a very difficult thing to acquire the virtue of charity. It is easy to be passive and docile, but it is terribly difficult to be really obedient. It is easy to be self-depreciating, but it is hard to be humble. We are constantly and consistently misled by reading as virtues and vices things which are merely dimensions of personality. Vice has to be acquired as much as virtue but it is a little easier to acquire it. There is no such thing as innate viciousness any more than there is such a thing as innate virtue. The child is not born into the world with built-in disobedience or lying habits.

The child comes into the world with a particular type of genetic inheritance and this means he has a special temperament. The second set of factors determining personality begins to take effect and these factors are persons. The child first experiences his mother who is his total world; later the father begins to play his part; at a third stage other children; at a fourth, other adults; and finally, a group of his peers. In all cultures and societies there is a definable, predictable sequence of interpersonal relationships. Second only to the genes, if indeed it is second, is this influence of other people. The set of interpersonal relations which the child experiences is almost equal in importance in determining the quality of his personality. The quality of the experience of being "you" is much more a function of your experience, of your parents, other children, adults, in the first two and a half years of your life than anything else that happened to you ever since. It would be very difficult to exaggerate the importance of these first few years. Your becoming "you" is a linear continuity through the phases of maturation.

Stages of Maturation

The first of these stages of maturation is the gestation period. The second phase is infancy up to about one and a half or two. The third phase is that of childhood which goes from two up to nine or ten, and this is divided into two sections. The first half is the relatively difficult stage from about two, two and a half up to four or five. The second half is a relatively placid period. The first half is the period during which the child begins to handle his internal emotional life. He does not make the grade unless he learns to do this. That is why it is so important.

The second half of childhood is the period when the emotional life subsides and the child becomes much more out-going. The world absorbs him, other people absorb him. What is the difference? In the first two years or so, the child's emotional life is quite straightforward, being simply a two-way street: he loves and is loved; he is frustrated, hates, gets angry, etc. At two, two and a half or three, the child becomes capable of envy, desire, acting a part. The infant is incapable of this. The child of three will snuggle up to his mother and put on a warm-hearted, affectionate act to gain something in return. He can play one parent against the other; he can inflict pain on another child to manipulate the other's behavior. This is an enormous advance on the first two years. It means the child is being determined from within by volatile emotions which he does not understand and he must come to terms with them. The importance of the third, fourth, and fifth years is that now for the first time the child begins to control his emotional life.

The next phase of childhood is rather quiet and peaceful, but around about nine or nine and a half, the child enters another phase. This is the pre-pubertal phase of emotional expansion. Puberty, the physiological onset of adolescence, is occurring earlier and earlier. About two years before the physiological onset, the child becomes psychologically pubertal, beginning to experience a renewed internal, expanded emotional life, expanded in range and depth. This parallels the expansion in range and depth of emotion at two, two and a half or three. Many of the infantile patterns of behavior appropriate to that age level are now re-enacted by the nine- to ten-year-old. For example, the child of three will lie on the floor in a tantrum when he is frustrated, and in the same way, the nine-year-old, unable to cope with the new expanded dimensions of his emotional life, may burst into a fit of anger or a flood of tears in an attempt to handle the internal emotions. This may carry on right up to thirteen, fourteen, or later.

The other parallel between the child of three or four and nine or ten is this: up to about three, the child has been behaving reasonably as far as the mother is concerned— when he is hungry she feeds him, when she puts him to bed he falls asleep. He does what she wants and she equates this with obedience. At about three and a half or four, the child starts saying, "No." He won't go to bed; he won't eat, etc., and the mother calls this disobedience. She wonders what has happened to the child who before was so obedient. She finds that he even tells lies. But how old does a child have to be before he is either disobedient or tells a lie? Being disobedient or telling lies is quite mature behavior. The child of four is incapable of such behavior. These are matters of character, and the mother has not yet recognized that what she is observing is temperament. In the same way, at nine or ten the child will re-enact this four-year-old negativism, just as he will re-enact the childish tantrums. The teacher instructs a child of seven or eight who makes reasonable progress and then suddenly she discovers she cannot teach the child a thing. He will refuse to do his homework. This is negativism.

These are two phases of childhood we do not know enough about, however they are very important from the viewpoint of personality. From the viewpoint of the religious life their importance lies in this: the tantrums and negativism will both be re-enacted at the next critical phase, the formation of the young religious. We all bear within us the infant and the child and the adolescent we were as these are all parts of our personality. The child at the age of six months begins the process of identifying with his father, the mother having been his total world during those first six months. From this time, until he is eighteen months to two years, the child absorbs the father's image as well as that of the mother, this becoming part of his personality. A great deal depends on the quality of those two images for the subsequent phases of development. Suppose the mother is cold and rejecting, a bit off-hand, incapable of giving needed warmth and security to the child. Suppose the father, instead of being a source of strength and comfort, is experienced as a threat, insecurity, instability. Suppose the father's handling of rewards and punishments is inconsistent. The child is absorbing all this, building into himself this rejection by the mother and the father's inconsistency, and for the rest of his life you will be able to identify in that child's personality some of the residual effects of that kind of infantile experience. Suppose in the case of another child, the mother is warm and affectionate, the father a source of strength and comfort, consistency and security. The second child in adolescence or adulthood will have a much easier task than the first in such matters as faith, worship, morals. In the formation of young religious, temperament, personality, and character factors have to be understood thoroughly. Early infantile and pre-adolescent and adolescent influences will come to the surface and affect the individual in ways that we have yet to learn a great deal about.

Another function that turns you into what you are now is your own personal experience of life and the world, the whole of the learning process that you have passed through. There is no innate knowledge in the human mind, not even knowledge of right or wrong. Every single thing you know had to be learned and this took place in many ways. Obviously, the world you experienced as a child, the emotions you felt, the educational opportunities, all these went into making you what you are. Without learning, without developing the intellect, the personality can never mature. That is why the mentally defective child, the mentally ill cannot become completely mature persons as the raw material is lacking.

Self-Initiated Acts

There is still another dimension that makes you "you." This is the area of. self-initiated acts, the behavior that you initiated yourself. Long before we can talk about responsibility we can talk about self-initiated behavior. The child at the age of three months, six months, nine months, initiates behavior of various kinds, reaching for a colored ball, moving around in his crib, beginning to crawl. These acts are self-initiated, but they are not responsible. Later on, the range of these acts widens enormously.

The infant and the child must experience "self" as well as building it up. If we never give him a chance to initiate behavior, he will never experience "self." The area in which you really experience yourself is that of decision-making and initiating acts. This is the existential proposition which teaches that you have created your "self." What comes into the world is a bundle of genes. Your environment and your experiences turn you into a human being and socialize you, turning you into the person you ought to be. In existentialist terminology: existence precedes essence. This is rather inaccurate terminology, but its meaning is correct. What is meant is that you exist as a person and then you make your choices, creating your personality by your self-initiated acts. This is the quality of being "you" in the moral sense. It begins long before we can legitimately begin to talk about moral acts as such, or character, but without it there can be no moral acts.

Suppose you were anxious about your child's welfare and you had some kind of omnipotent power whereby you could say, I can control this child for life; I can assure his going to heaven. I can do this by keeping him in isolation. Would you be entitled to do this or to think along these lines? The answer is no. It would be equivalent to murder because it would be the destruction of his personality. Why? Because you would be eliminating the very things that make the child human, namely, the capacity to perform self-initiated acts, the making of decisions, choice, free behavior, commitment. You would be turning the child into a vegetable.

Youngsters entering religious life today have had opportunities for decision-making and commitment which were not the cultural norm a generation ago. The Council has taught us, and hence we no longer have any option here, that we must take into account the psychological and cultural dimensions of the world from which our vocations are coming. Here, then, is the crux of the problem—the youngsters have been growing as persons, their personality has developed and expanded in a most enriching way, and even a worshipful way because they show forth God's glory by being what they are. Then they find themselves in a situation where it appears that this kind of growth stops; they seemingly have to become passive and docile. Self-initiated acts and choices are more or less eliminated from their world. A great many feel frustrated; they feel they are not fulfilling themselves as persons; the self-realization which ought to be their goal is now being denied them and as a result they leave.

In the formative years, there are two things to bear in mind in order to develop their personality. One is that we must be able to teach them to experience "self." The other, we must maximize self-initiated acts and choices. This is taking place in some communities, but perhaps in the past we did not realize the need for these two things. Unless you have the time to be alone, it is very difficult to experience your "self." We should try to build a great deal more "aloneness" in these early years.

The second dimension, the self-initiated acts, presents a great difficulty since there must be public order, social life, community, etc. The question is whether or not we are approaching the personality in the right way through the community, social demands, the rule. The current problems, the tensions of obedience-authority, for example, are frequently due more to our mistaken notions of obedience than to the young people's false notions of authority. Unless we realize that obedience, being a virtue cannot be acquired passively but only actively, and unless our young persons in formation can see that obeying is active choosing, then they will not understand the moral nature of authority.

Let us define what maturity would be if we achieved it. It would be the end-result of the functions we have just outlined. The genetic processes would have led us to an adequate functioning as organisms. Our early experience with parents, children, adults, would have led us to a reasonably balanced mental health, and mental health can almost be defined as good interpersonal relations. The learning processes would have led us to a reasonable cultivation of the talents God endowed us with, a reasonable intellectual outlook on the world and an understanding of our role. Self-initiated acts would have led us to have formed a well-balanced, more or less virtuous type of character.

6. THE PSYCHOLOGY OF ADOLESCENCE

Let us consider for a while the psychology of adolescence so that we can obtain more insight into the personalities of those we are supposed to form. Modern adolescence commences earlier and ends later than that of former generations. Noteworthy is the fact that adolescence in our culture is very different from adolescence of a generation ago or from that of other cultures. We must not assume that because today's adolescent is different, therefore he is more difficult, somewhat less formed, and less valuable. In fact he may be far more valuable than his counterpart of the last generation. Since every culture produces its own appropriate vocations, we must assume theologically that the Holy Spirit will evoke vocations from this culture at this time.

Self-Identity

It used to be thought that the adolescent's main problem was one of sexuality. Those who have studied the matter have discovered that this is not so. The primary problem of youth today is the problem of self-identity, of coming to an appropriate level of self-knowledge. For the child this is an easy task. When the child wonders: Who am I? What am I? he is told: You are John and you are a little boy. For the adolescent the answer is not that easy. In addition to the problem of self-identity there is also that of role or status. In a comparatively simple and unchanging society the adolescent role is clearly defined: he is to obey, to be dependent, to learn a limited number of skills. He is not an adult and consequently he is treated as a child. In a rapidly changing and highly developed society the problem of identity and role become acute. Our young people have real problems in these areas. There was a time when seventeen to nineteen meant the termination of adolescence; however, in our culture this now lasts up to about twenty-six and later. In a more stable and less developed culture persons were entering religious life who had resolved their identity crisis. They had come to an appropriate level of self-identification, appropriate of course for that culture. They were not as yet adults but had no real conflicts about who or what they were.

Why is this problem so acute today? It is because we have operated through the adolescent years on a basis guaranteed to reduce identity and enhance conformity. We are stimulating the child to lose his/her identity in group activity so that he rarely has a chance to come to terms with himself. School, camps in the summer, recreational facilities, organizations of all kinds, all these group-processes tend to render the identity problem more difficult to solve. The notion of conformity is constantly projected on youth. Certainly these youngsters have an opportunity to explore their talents which was not possible to those of a generation ago. Nevertheless they still have not resolved satisfactorily where these talents lie, what their potential is, what their optimal level of functioning is, hence they have a problem.

Secondly, the role problem is present. What is an adolescent in our culture? The young person is simultaneously dependent and independent. Vast areas of his/her life are at their own disposal and this is good and extremely valuable. However it does mean an unresolved conflict as to whether one is dependent or independent. Perhaps the best way to understand this is to consider the question of the sixteen to seventeen-year-old girl. She asks her father for the key to the house. She begs that all restraints be removed, telling him she will be back at night when she pleases and will go where she pleases. Here her independence is coming to the fore. She has been granted a great deal of this in her choice of clothing, recreation, personal friends, etc. The question is, does she really want the restraints removed? Or is she really a dependent person frightened by that kind of freedom? When one examines the question one finds that she really is not seeking this total freedom. What she really is asking for is the right conceded to her of asking for the key. Whether she gets it or not is secondary to the fact that she wants the right to ask for it. With reference to her coming back when she pleases, she will come back at eleven o'clock when asked but on condition that she is not to feel guilty if she does not. It is not the returning home at a stipulated hour that hurts, but that she is being told to do so or else. This conflicts with the independence she already enjoys in other matters. She is still dependent and basically frightened at having all the restraints removed.

Adolescents need limits and the problem is how to set those limits. It must be resolved not by imposing limits but by activating the individual's choice so that one imposes the limits on oneself. This is the essence of human freedom and we have forgotten this with respect to the subject-superior relationship. Limits imposed from without are not necessarily sanctifying. They become so when the person accepts them willingly.

Role Learning

The role of the young is ambiguous, dependent and independent. There is still another dimension in which this role is ambiguous. In a relatively stable society the difference between boys and girls is sharply defined from infancy. In adolescence the segregation and differentiation is still more marked, the girl gradually learning the feminine role from her mother, the boy, from his father, male teachers, etc. In our society the feminine-masculine roles have become blurred. The girl does not learn from her mother and the boy does not learn from his father. In the educational process the roles overlap so that it is almost impossible to distinguish any differentiation. Recreational facilities blur the distinction still further. All this is bound to produce confusion. This is not bad but very good. Why? Because our role separation in the past, looked upon as of divine intervention, is now understood as a product of its time, a cultural artefact. In that time of clearcut distinctions we believed, for instance, that girls were not good at mathematics, but we realize now that this is false. The learning capacity of either sex is identical, the difference lying only in the teacher's ability to instruct them. There is no difference in the sexes regarding engineering, and in the future we shall have a number of women engineers. We have already accepted women doctors. We accept women pilots. In other words, the male-female role is biologically distinct but the masculine-feminine roles are not.

The girl entering the religious life today will not represent the feminine role accepted in the past. She will not be the docile, subordinate type her grandmother was. There is no such thing as natural docility, subordination, or dependence in women as these things are only cultural artefacts. They do not belong to woman as such and as long as we think they should we are going to be wondering what has become of the new generation. We shall be judging them as too independent and too impossible to form. They are simply the products of their times and culture. We should recognize women as totally capable of most of the traditionally masculine skills.

What is the relevance of all this to personality development in the religious life? First, the youngster may be entering too soon, at an age appropriate in another culture when the identity crisis was resolved. If the young person has not resolved this crisis, if he or she does not know who he is, he will be incapable of making the choice necessary for a commitment. We recognize in the vacillation of young religious before temporary or final vows that their problem is not whether or not they should make vows. Their problem is that they don't know who they are or what they are doing.

A hundred years ago, when primary education was still a luxury and universal literacy was not yet the cultural norm, we were happy to accept youngsters and put them through the levels of education, allowing them to grow into the religious life. Later on we took them at the end of their primary education when that had become the cultural norm, and later on still, we took them after they had completed high school. During this period some Congregations still accepted the young and gave them their high school training. They passed through the juniorate and then entered the novitiate. This has become very unusual today. We wait now for the completion of their secondary education and then put them through college and university levels, giving them teacher-training or some form of professional skill.

We may ask ourselves, in view of the cultural changes, is it not time to begin thinking of accepting them only after they have completed their college education? Since the identity crisis is not resolved for many until then, perhaps this is the only solution.

With reference to the role or status problem we can consider it this way. For those of one or two generations ago it was fairly simple to be a seminarian or a sister. These had already resolved many problems and their role was clearly defined. One knew then what it was to be masculine or feminine. The adolescent today is confused because we are still operating a stereotype of masculinity-femininity accepted twenty or even ten years ago. We may still be demanding conformity to that stereotype while the young person is incapable of changing from the present cultural definitions of masculinity or femininity. We may be trying to form their personality along one axis while it is moving along another. We may also be pressuring them in such a way that we are not producing good religious and may be losing good vocations.

There is still another consideration. In response to the Church's demands we must give a college or university level of formation to many so that they may carry out their mission as "salt of the earth." We realize from research among sisters that there is a constant shift in personality from traditional feminine roles to more masculine attitudes and outlooks as a result of training. There is a dilemma here. To produce the type of religious the Church desires and the People of God need we are going to find marked changes in his/her personality and we run the risk of thinking this is a loss rather than a gain.

If we were to list traditional masculine/feminine attitudes, what would be placed on the feminine list? One might probably think of the following: sensitivity, docility, defensive withdrawal, domesticity, etc. On the other side of the scale, under masculinity, one might put: leadership, strength, autonomy, insensitivity. What happens when one continues education into college and university levels? Every girl thus educated tends to move across the scale closer to the traditionally masculine dimensions of personality and, to a certain extent, vice versa. Instead of docility she is ready to take on leadership; instead of passivity, activity; instead of dependence, independence; instead of sensitivity, a great deal more apparent insensitivity. It would be ridiculous to say these are undesirable traits. This is part of the cultural change. It makes the formation problem more difficult and more acute.

It will mean that the young person will be less likely to identify with the older group. In the past less mature girls were able to identify with the mother-figure, the Novice-Mistress, Mother Superior, Mother General. Now the candidates are the types who have moved across the scale towards masculinity, but whose identity within themselves is not even resolved as yet. These will find it more difficult to identify with the older group for several reasons. Firstly, by so doing they will have lost their identity to that extent just as adolescents do when conforming to a group. Secondly, they see the older members of the community as representing a style of femininity from which they have withdrawn in favor of more traditionally "masculine" traits.

The task of formation becomes more difficult still if we think we must form the young according to our own image. It is inevitable that we ourselves will be their model. We may be the wrong model, not in every respect but in some important respects. We might be asking an identification with ourselves that is impossible and because of this the young person leaves the religious life. If we could only recognize their value as individuals, helping them seek and find their own identity, giving them a model they can imitate, we might succeed in producing valuable persons.

Cultural Values

Contemporary cultural values should be added to our picture of the adolescent. The adolescent values of the nineteen-twenties were perhaps childish. The boy of fifteen in those days would have been satisfied to own a watch, travel on a train, etc. Take note of the change in values today. How many of the young would willingly give up any form of education at seventeen? Their ambition is to go to college. Intellectual values are part of their world. Many of them have a real appreciation of the arts. Many of them listen intelligently to music and read books and appreciate poetry in ways their predecessors could not. In fact, it was customary to despise these values in a former generation. How many adolescents of thirty years ago had a world-view of social problems? Now this is the normal occupation of a great deal of their time. How many young people thirty years ago would have gone on long trips in the summer? Thousands start off on their own today.

In other words, the young entering religious life today will already have had an exposure to a much wider world, to an intellectual excitement, to an aesthetic experience which we did not enjoy. It is this type we shall be getting and we must recognize that they are equipped with valuable assets which we must not allow to atrophy. This is equivalent to burying their talents. These people are culturally more mature than we were at the same age. The major effect of college or university education is to retard emotional maturity and prolong the period of adolescence. We may be doing the same thing in novitiates and houses of study. If so, we should not be surprised to find that their behavior does not change substantially during the few years we are trying to form them.

What do we obtain on the debit side of adolescence? First, there is the tendency of the adolescent to avoid him/herself, doing almost anything rather than have this confrontation. When alone they will easily get absorbed in daydreaming, losing themselves in a world of fantasy. By not providing the kind of "aloneness" mentioned earlier and by prolonging adolescence upward we exclude the possibility of the adolescent's self experience. We have tried to teach them something about behavior and perhaps we are concentrating too much on this. This is true of spiritual books. For too long these have been concerned with items of behavior such as acquiring particular virtues and avoiding particular vices. This is not said in a condemnatory way, but today there is a tendency to move away from that. Spiritual books now deal with the person's activity in his/her interpersonal relationship with God. In my examination of conscience, as long as I am concerned with items of behavior, e.g., what did I do? I can dodge confrontation with myself. Remember that self-knowledge is the first step to maturity. The old Greek saying: "know thyself" and St. Augustine's prayer: "Lord, that I may know myself and that I may know thee" are two important elements in the spiritual life.

Secondly, on the debit side adolescents rarely know how

to handle their emotional life. They have not learned to control their emotional responses and when they manage to control them it may not be rational and certainly will not be mature control. It may be repression, a technical term which means a defence arising out of fear. An adolescent is often frightened by his/her emotional life. And the young person coming into the novitiate may very well be operating a defence process of repression. By prolonging adolescence upward we may make it unnecessary for them to acquire control over their emotional life. Later on when the defence of repression fails, as it inevitably will, they must confront the problem of self, their instinctual life, their sexuality, all at one time, perhaps in the late twenties and early thirties. Instead of having taught them a mature control process we may have allowed them to coast along on repressive, defencive functions. Then when the storm arises, they find themselves powerless. Repression is not virtue. The virtue of chastity for example, is really acquired only by a very mature person who has learned a new and positive way of loving.

Again, adolescents may have recourse to suppression to handle the problem of their emotional life. This is rarer than repression. It means that the young person acquires a bland, detached, calm exterior, walking through life unruffled by anything, self-possessed, "cool" to use the modern expression. This is suppression, not control. It is predicated on the contemporary cultural norm that you must not get excited about things and so the first thing to suppress is your emotions. Such persons are more vulnerable than are those who have recourse to repression because suppression just cannot work and will eventually lead to explosion.

7. EMOTIONAL MATURITY

Psychological maturity can be dated from the point where certain processes are recognized in the individual. The first of these is the point where emotional control has been established; this is not a sudden occurrence but a long process. The second characteristic of maturity is the acceptance of responsibility for one's acts to the limits of their foreseeable consequences. The third is the realization by the individual of his autonomy and uniqueness as a person.

Control

The notion of control is the point where one experiences in an appropriate degree an appropriate emotion so that one's behavior determines one's emotions, not vice versa. When emotion completely determines behavior we are acting as infants; when it is a major determinant we are acting as adolescents. Part of the formation for maturity and personality development must lie in teaching emotional control.

The adolescent attempts to handle emotion by repression or suppression. Control of emotions is a high-level activity and does not mean running away from them through fear which is repression or by denying their existence which is suppression. It means a balanced moderation such as St. Paul speaks about: "Rejoice with those who rejoice, weep with those who weep..." (Rm 12:15). The appropriateness of the emotion is the first dimension. In the past we have conveyed to the young the idea that emotions should be suppressed. This may have worked with the docile, plastic, and malleable characters who were ready to be submissive. But today what we must do is teach the young to recognize that emotions are good, but must be kept under control and the first point is moderation.

The second point is the appropriateness of the emotion. This, too, is part of control. For instance, the person experiencing a paralyzing panic at having to read in public has not achieved control; again, the religious who becomes sad and depressed because of a superior's reprimand is exhibiting an inappropriate level of emotion; one getting excessively angry because things go wrong physically is also immature. The question of moderation and appropriateness are both dimensions of this control.

Emotional control is possible, thirdly, only through an understanding of and insight into one's emotional life. We should be prepared to teach young people some levels of insight, giving them a good deal of psychology in the first years of their religious life. Should we fail to impart this knowledge we shall discover they are handling emotion in unhealthy ways. Mental health and maturity are the same thing. Among these unhealthy ways are the obvious ones. There is the young sister who has recourse to violent fits of sobbing when depressed or lonely; or there is the brother who converts his emotional upsets into physical symptoms. Such a person is not mentally ill but very immature. I want to keep the mental illness category distinct from the mental health/maturity category. The brother who finds some of his emotions difficult to handle may convert them into such symptoms as headaches and backaches. This is easily understood if we remember that most of us, having had to face examinations, experienced the marked somatic reaction called the "sinking feeling." Anxiety is here converted into nausea, the simple conversion of an emotion into a physical symptom. We may not recognize this and send for a doctor. He may not recognize it and prescribe tablets. The aches may clear up but another set of symptoms is likely to appear. The whole organism becomes the subject of the conversion of emotions into various physical symptoms. Teaching a good deal of insight into the emotional life can eliminate that kind of escape route from the immature person's world.

The immature person cannot face decision-making. To avoid this and being too immature to talk it out, the person speaks through the organism which has a language of its own. In this the person is acting as a child. When a child has a discomfort, the organism makes the protest because the child cannot verbalize what irritates it. The mother often interprets the disturbance and makes the appropriate adjustment. You will find young people doing this in novitiates too. With regard to doubts about vocation, the mature person will be quite capable of talking it out, making a decision, and following it through, even if it may mean leaving. The immature person may keep saying: "Yes, I believe I have a vocation." We are sometimes trapped into accepting this oral language and neglecting the organic language. The immature individual who protests that she wants to be a sister but whose organism is speaking a different language should be told to leave. Very often we help them over their organic symptoms and then, perhaps eight or ten years later, when the person has matured sufficiently to recognize her difficulty she will either opt out or cause trouble.

Emotional control is vital to maturity. We can teach it only when we have it ourselves. If we find our attitudes, judgments, and evaluations are colored by feelings, then we have not attained control. If we find that we are prone to unpredictable depressions, anxieties, explosions of anger, then we have no control. Those who must appoint superiors, mistresses of novices, etc., should take great care that those appointed have control.

Responsibility

The second dimension of maturity is the capacity to accept responsibility for one's acts to the uttermost limits of their foreseeable consequences. This is a very mature process. You will understand its importance if you look back at the child and the adolescent. The child of four to six does not have this type of responsibility. The adolescent begins to have it but tries to shelve it. When he has done something wrong he will try to push off responsibility by different devices. Even adults are tempted to do the same. Adam in the book of Genesis blamed the woman; the woman blamed the serpent. Cain asks: "Am I my brother's keeper?" (Gn 3:12). Right through life we try to do this. The adolescent's device is: "Everybody is doing it so I am not responsible." This is how the immature person acts especially when in a group and even in a formation group. They may be responsible as a group, but the mature person will understand that being responsible as a group also means individual responsibility. We have to raise this sense of responsibility more and more and train each to accept it to the limit of the foreseeable consequences. We cannot say: "I did that but did not intend this effect." If it was a foreseeable consequence, then we as mature persons must say: "Yes, I am responsible for that."

Autonomy

The third dimension of emotional maturity is the most difficult of all, that is, learning to accept one's total isolation as a person. This is where responsibility really comes in. There are two dangers in forming the young. First, the danger of misreading the notion expressed by St. Paul concerning the Mystical Body: "...so we, though many, are one body in Christ, and individually members one of another" (Rm 12:5). Secondly, the danger of misreading the role and function of community.

Many have been misled by John Donne's "No Man is an Island." He was stressing that we are all related to one another in countless ways. We have misread him as though he were saying that somehow we are parts of the same organism and we have thought that this was the Mystical Body in action. It is not true that "no man is an island." We are all islands and our only communication is through external signs. We attempt to sink our identities in each other in all sorts of peculiar ways. The mature person does not do this, for he recognizes that personality is defined by its incommunicability, the total isolation of each person as an entity on its own. Here the term "autonomy" is preferable though it is frequently misunderstood. Maturity is achieved only when one deliberately accepts one's total isolation with the consequential autonomy this implies and the responsibility with which one goes to God.

What about St. Paul's "members of one another"? It is only in the life of grace that we are members one of another. The membership is not part of our experienced world any more than is grace. It is a reality, but its reality is a mystery, for it does not diminish our isolation. The mature person learns that this is not something to fear but something to be achieved. He knows that an interchange is essential for the proper functioning of society. He knows also that as a person he is uniquely responsible, isolated, autonomous.

Part of this misunderstanding comes from community life. Obviously in community we are all related to each other in many ways so that the community can act as a unit. The danger lies in subordinating the individual to the community's well-being. We must not lose sight of the fact that the community is a means to the person's well-being. The community as such, however, does not go to God for eternity. Presumably and hopefully, we shall constitute a community in heaven, but it is only in isolation that we reach the vision of God, not in groups. It is part of maturity to see the difference between community and person and not get the values mixed. This is especially the case with young people. Often they see, in their search for identity and maturity, the community as a blocking mechanism. They say they cannot bear to go on, to live their lives as non-persons, as one of a group. They have misunderstood the relationship of persons to the community, or have been taught incorrectly what this is. Sometimes we are reluctant to face up to what the correct relationship is.

The original construction of the religious life, the family of St. Benedict, was based on the family in the West at the time he created this form of life. It was not the nuclear family of the father-mother-children, but the three tiered, many faceted relationship of the extended family. We continued to emphasize this family concept when the nuclear family had taken the place of the more primitive or extended family. In our thinking, we still look upon the superior and subjects as parents and children. Whether we like it or not we shall find that this is the model operative in most people's minds. As long as we think this way we are going to fall into the trap into which many mothers fall. A mother will watch her girl grow up and reach the age of eleven, twelve, thirteen, and all is well. When her dawning adolescence begins to demand a certain autonomy, certain relationships outside the family, the wise mother encourages this and in so doing she binds the child to herself more closely. The girl comes back describing her experiences and there is a shared relationship. The unwise mother becomes disturbed and tries to curb outside influences. She binds the child, she thinks, closer by keeping her home, but in fact she is alienating her. She is holding her back from maturity. Sometimes superiors are frightened at the notion of mature, autonomous, leadership-exercising persons as members of a community. The reason for this is that all the devices of running a community are geared to some elements of dependence and immaturity. This is changing rapidly. In terms of changes taking place in communities of religious women from the feminine stereotype across the spectrum to the masculine side, we are going to obtain a great many mature and autonomous persons. The problem will be not to hold them back and make them docile subjects, but to reconstruct community life so that they can be given their status as adults and still live in community. It will require a great deal more insight than we have already achieved.

Clearly, not all will reach this stage. The Holy Spirit can produce vocations from any sector of society and we shall continue to receive dependent and immature persons. This does not mean we should define the goal that way. We must define it in terms of the optimal functioning of the very best members of the community. It is not that these should be regarded as extraordinary and the others as normal, rather the former should be taken as normal and the others, the immature, dependent ones as the exceptions.

Some problems arise. One is the exercise of authority. There must be authority in the religious life as in any form of society. The first thing to note is that authority differs from power. Authority is moral. This does not mean that it always binds in conscience which is a different concept altogether. Any form of interpersonal relationship where people are related to each other as persons such as parent to child, teacher to pupil, management to workers, is an authority relationship. It is based on the fact that the acts of one person will be expected to have an effect on those of another person. This is a moral relationship. It may not bind in conscience, nevertheless it is still moral. Power is a different matter. The state has power to compel the citizen to behave in this way and not that way. The policeman has the power to control a mob, but he has authority to control traffic. When he raises his hand and cars stop, he exercises authority; if he uses a stick to quell a mob, he is using power.

As the ethos of the Church changes we find a radical change in the concept of authority. I say radical. Up to Vatican II we thought of the structure of authority in the Church as a pyramid, the pope on top and a line of command clearly defined going down through metropolitans, archbishops, bishops, pastors, curates, and the faithful. It was conceived of as a hierarchical structure. The idea that there was a democratic process involved would have been rejected by many up to 1964. When I say there is a democratic process involved I do not mean the Church is a democracy, but rather that what has happened is that authority is now seen as being even more effective when operated in a democratic manner instead of being exercised in an authoritarian way. Leadership of all kinds is changing in this way. It goes right through the structure of society, but the most interesting thing is the democratization of the use of ecclesiastical authority.

Structures and functions within the Church echo those of the surrounding society. This is the case with regard to vocations, the family, the notion of community. It is part of the eternal dialectic of the relationship of the People of God to the rest of the world. It was inevitable then that as society at large and the culture changed toward democratization, this would happen within the Church. This change in society happens because of a cultural change that precedes it. In other words, people rise higher in their status as persons through cultural influences to which they are subject. As they rise higher the democratization of authority becomes possible, then desirable, then effective. Superiors are wielding their authority in a much more democratic way. It still is a moral authority and as such essentially unchanged, however its mode of implementation is radically changed.This is inevitable and will cause tension and conflict. Change is always difficult to adjust to, but let us not worry about the tensions and conflicts. Another dimension of maturity is precisely the capacity to live with them successfully. It is not the function of maturity to get rid of them.

8. MASCULINE-FEMININE PSYCHOLOGY

It is clear that men and women differ in certain definable respects—biologically, psychologically, psychoculturally. The last mentioned dimension means the attitudes, values, aspirations, and ideas set up by the existing culture. Many of these attitudes are variable and it is a danger signal for a culture when they solidify. When they are no longer flexible and are confused with natural and connatural dimensions of our personality it is a bad sign. This has happened in our Western culture.

Unreal Stereotypes

The biological differences between the sexes are not our concern here. We are not denying their importance, but what is important about these differences is that they are frequently made the basis for arguments concerning psychological and psychocultural differences. We have the experience now of women soldiers, astronauts, athletes, so there is no biological foundation for the stereotype of woman as the "weaker sex." No woman has run a mile in four minutes, but neither did any man until the last decade. It is worth remembering that women outlive men.

When considering psychological differences we meet another traditional stereotype. In the past, it was thought that girls were not good at mathematics, that they had a lower I.Q. The popular attitude could be described as a belief that there are fewer girls than boys in the upper intelligence brackets and that girls' intelligence is more intuitive than rational. All the evidence shows the same distribution of intelligence, the same range of aptitudes. The differences we assumed to be innate are in fact psychocultural artefacts. If one could change the stereotype, the expectation is that girls or boys would change. In the fields of philosophy, engineering, politics, where there is a preponderance of men over women, we must not assume that there is a male dimension involved. The pressures of our society have so emphasized that women go one way, men another, that at the end of the line we find them separated and then think this difference is inborn.

The psychologist attempts to see through these dimensions of the stereotype and penetrate further into the minds of men and women to see if there is any inner difference that might be regarded as a sexually based or differentiated variable. He does this by a variety of techniques—interviews, inventories, rating scales, questionnaires, all the paraphernalia at his disposal. He analyzes his results and interprets them.

We all have an image of ourselves, but independently of this image we have a self-image of our role as male or female. It is clear that there are devices currently used by society to convey a particular self-image or sex self-image. From an early age girls are taught they should be more fastidious than boys. "Sugar and spice and all things nice, that's what girls are made of." The boys were "made of frogs and snails and puppy dogs' tails." This is not given to children as a true proposition, but as a way of conveying an affective tone, an emotional attitude. The realities of little girls' aggression, cruelty, sadism, selfishness, a distaste for dolls and a desire to be a tomboy, all these are ignored in the attitudes we attempt to convey to the child. So he or she is gradually taught a different set of attitudes, values, controls. The girl's self-image changes in the direction of the social expectations and determinants, and by five or six she preens herself in pretty frocks or begins to admire herself in the mirror. By seven little girls are aware of their femininity just as little boys are aware of their masculinity, not by any innate knowledge but by the kind of attitudes we convey in subtle ways. By nine or ten their self-image changes again. The girl withdraws, becoming a little more silent. At the onset of puberty the image of her sexual role becomes clearer. This is really the point where femininity emerges perhaps for the first time as a fully clarified concept. It is often forgotten that girls are much closer to biological realities than are boys. The girl will always be much more of a mystery to the boy than vice versa. She soon learns the importance of perpetuating this mystery. She begins to "put across" her essential femininity.

The adolescent in today's world is undergoing profound changes due to the far-reaching cultural and sociological changes occurring in our environment. It is because of these changes that woman's self-image is changing. The stereotype woman of Victorian society has already disappeared, but even the elements of stability represented by that stereotype are also changing and—let us put it bluntly—for the better. It is a greater tribute to women that they are being acknowledged today as full human persons in all respects than was the apparent respect given them when they were regarded as the "weaker sex," the dependent, subordinate group. Nobody really believes the Victorian stereotype, but few can formulate an alternative and fewer still would accept an alternative if we were to produce one. We are all afraid of losing something valuable by changing an accepted self-image. Yet it has changed. What has changed is not womanhood but the feminine role.

Masculine-Feminine Roles

A role is an internally consistent pattern of ways of behaving in response to anticipated stimuli, in this case the behavior of others. The pattern of behavior so established governs our interpersonal relationship with other members, either of our own or another society. This is more cleverly put by Shakespeare: "All the world's a stage and each man in his time plays many parts." This "playing a part" is not acting hypocritically. It really means learning how to be what one ought to be. This role is not an assumed role, not a facade, a mask, but learning how to be what we are in any case, how to realize our potentialities. Girls must learn how to be girls and boys, how to be boys. There is no innate knowledge of how a girl or boy ought to behave. The masculine-feminine role has to be learned. One of the problems of the formation of the young is that we teach them a particular role in terms of inherited stereotypes whereas the role society expects is different. They find this conflicting. They must be taught the role they have to fulfill, not the one we have unconsciously identified as the only or most desirable role.

Roles have changed. The role of a woman in a primitive society is obviously different from that in a more economically viable society. In a relatively stable society the roles of the sexes are solidified, clearcut. A girl was expected to share with her mother in certain activities, acquiring certain skills at the highest level she could and carrying them out in this way. The same for the boy. He was to be the bread-winner. This is not true in our sophisticated society. The role of woman in the family, local government and public life have changed radically in our own time. It is because these roles have changed that what we understand by masculinity and femininity has changed.

The essential thing about roles is that they have to be learned. If there were an innate knowledge as to how to fulfill one or the other role, things would be easier, but less pleasing and exciting. The female role, the biologically determined role, is not variable. Because of this we tended to think of the feminine role as invariable. While the female role is organically and biologically conditioned, the feminine role is not simply a function of organic dimensions. Some men are "feminine" just as some women are "masculine." The role determination is not totally identifiable with the biological reality. It was said of St. Teresa of Avila by her bishop that she should have been a man. He was thinking of the role she was enacting as it differed from the typically feminine role of her times. Nowadays it would be regarded as perfectly normal, acting as she was in an out-going, creative way. The bishop thought this was masculine, and did not see it simply as a dimension of her personality rather than of her sex. The feminine role in our times has become much more goal-choosing, self-directing, leadership-exercising than was ever the case in any culture.

Social Status

Linked with role is the concept of status. The subordinate status of women in the past was based on social expectations, but by a kind of reciprocal causality the status also created the social expectations. They were interlocked in a reciprocal relationship. This you find right through the history of Christianity. Despite the role of women in the gospel who followed our Lord, ministering to him, and despite the exalted position of our Lady, something of this alleged subordination was attributed to womanhood as such. The lower status of woman was probably due as much to impersonal, economic factors as to selfish male ones. By impersonal, economic factors I mean that women on the whole in underdeveloped societies were not a creative unit in the economy. The male was the creative unit and the female was the hewer of wood and drawer of water. She merely did what she was told. The male created the way of life of his people. This is no longer the case and because of this changed economic status the feminine role has likewise changed.

Another factor is the psychological, affective tone. This refers to the quality of being a woman as distinct from being a man. Since none of us can experience both it is difficult to talk about it. Nevertheless we have valuable clues to follow. Psychologists would probably agree with the following statement: the psychology of women implies or necessitates a high sensitivity, a more acute awareness of feelings, gentleness in attitudes, a receptivity to others. The reason this is true is that when we find a man acting this way we regard him either as effeminate or saintly. In other words, he is a male living at a high level of grace or he is not normal. We identify something in this affective tone as womanly. On the other hand, a woman who is insensitive is hardly looked upon as feminine. Masculinity as contrasted with femininity in this way involves a higher capacity for action, aggressiveness, lower sensitivity, and perhaps a marked tendency to form judgments independently of emotional factors. The male mind is often affected in its judgments by emotion, but a man tries more consciously than does the woman to come to a conclusion on evidence, not feelings. A man is less likely to say that he knows something is true because he "feels it in his bones."

If it is true that the formation of young sisters through college and university courses is moving them away from past typically feminine roles, we must not make the mistake of deploring this end-result. We should not say: "Let us give them what they should have in education and formation, but let us hope they will not end up the way they should end up as a result of this formation." You cannot have the means without the end, nor can you have a well-educated, mature girl without having some loss in the stereotype. This holds for novices. The formation you are giving them, if you have a clear idea of the end-result, will lead them away from the passive, docile, subordinate type of the past. You cannot retain these characteristics while at the same time trying to give them the other, more mature type of formation. We should learn to see their movement towards a more "masculine" dimension not as a loss but as a gain inasmuch as it means the disappearance of a purely socially and culturally determined stereotype which handicapped women and prevented them from giving their best.

Psychological Differences

There are certain differences between the sexes I have not touched upon. We know there are differences in occupational interests. Margaret Mead, the great cultural anthropologist, thought that all the differences were socially or psychoculturally determined. It is probable, however, that there are occupational interests which vary between male and female which are not matters of chance or socio-cultural determination. For example, occupational interests expressed by boys, adolescents, young men tend towards adventure, outdoor activity, scientific investigation, physical phenomena, the business world. Girls move towards the domestic, aesthetic, indoor occupations, the care of the young, the helpless, the distressed. This emerges in many studies investigating these interests. In their emotional reactions one gets consistent differences also. They are not part of the stereotype but part of the female person. A woman is compassionate, sympathetic, fastidious, more emotionally expressive, and much more severe a moralist. Although she is much more severe as a moralist she will still claim to have less control of her emotions. The male will claim more control but will not have it.

There are two complementary dimensions to being human—the male and the female. This does not imply that we have two types of human beings. Let us negate three propositions. First, there is no such thing as womanly intuition. Secondly, there is nothing necessarily fluffy about being a woman. Thirdly, there is nothing weak about the "weaker sex." Now let us state some positive propositions. The female dimensions of being a human person involve certain capacities, especially that of creativity, bringing forth much fruit. Secondly, she has the capacity to resonate emotionally in a way a man has not. She feels what the other person is feeling. This is mistakenly called "intuition." Thirdly, she has the ability to love without possessing. A man wants to love and possess the object loved. The woman has a much greater capacity to love without possessing the object loved. This often gets distorted and possessiveness is substituted for love, however this is a derogation from her status as woman, not a dimension of womanhood.

Much more than a man, a woman has to feel wanted. A man is happy to know his boss is not going to fire him because he is essential to the business. A woman needs to feel that in much the same way in which I spoke of her emotional resonance. It is not enough to say: "I want you to do this, sister." She must really feel that the superior who has given her the job really wants her. It is not a question of ambition. It is a very quiet sort of thing, just a little under the surface all the time. A woman has the capacity to desire objects and this intensely, but she also has within her a deep, objectless yearning. Gradually she finds the necessary objects on which to focus. A woman has a great capacity to confuse different internal states. She can really hate somebody and say: "Look, I don't hate you at all, I really love you, but...." Meanwhile she is seething with dislike. A man is much more likely to identify the real quality of his internal state. This is a problem because often the conflict between husband and wife is precisely due to this.

There is also a certain emotional lability in women. This means a diffusion of emotions from one quality into another, a spread between emotions, leaving no clearcut edge between one emotional quality and another. This is a very feminine thing. With a man the identifiable quality of emotion is clearcut: hate is not love, fear is not anger, desire is not repudiation. Emotional lability is a normal constituent of the woman and, in her, hate and love, fear and anger, desire and repulsion can intermingle and become confused. All these get mixed in a sort of global "mélange" of emotions instead of being an identifiable series of them.

Let us add a word about the feminine dimension of vocation. It is part of the specific quality of firmness and decision-making which is probably less marked in the boy. A young man goes to the seminary and on to the priesthood without experiencing the sort of agonizing over the finality of his decision that the girl experiences. This gives her a much more clearcut vocation in the end. There is a warmth radiated by the girl who chooses the vocation to the religious life, a warmth of love rarely seen in the male vocation.

A sister's feminine creativity which is the capacity to give creatively or to create by the very giving of herself may become stultified. Let us put this in the form of a question: Is not the feminine creativity which should specify the female vocation often channeled into non-productive ends? It very probably is. We call these things "recreational activity." They are creative in a secondary way, but they are not the sort of creativity which would give fulfillment to the femininity of the female vocation. A woman seeks security in the love of God which is not given to men. Men do not understand this feminine need in the vocation of religious. Because of the emotional lability described, even fear of the Lord becomes love and must be met by being aware that one is wanted. Very often superiors forming religious do not convey clearly enough this essential feeling of being wanted. "I will draw you with the bonds of Adam." This feeling must be conveyed. It is not a human love in the ordinarily accepted meaning of the term, but it is nevertheless human love. It is the human love in which the sister's personality can in fact become the "spouse of Christ." There must be that dimension of human love which, though not a felt, organic, biological love, is nevertheless a very real and human love—the love of one person for another.

The idea of "spouse" must be looked at carefully because it can become too anthropomorphic, and in some cases may involve the weaving of a rather unhealthy fantasy. Between husband and wife the relationship is, ideally, a mutual and reciprocal experience of felt-states of human desire, love and satisfaction. In the concept of the "spouse of Christ," however, the dimensions of desire and satisfaction are neither the constituents of the relationship nor the criteria by which she must evaluate it, but by her own loving and self-giving a sister must create the reality of the relationship.

9. THE MIDDLE AND DECLINING YEARS

With respect to the problem surrounding the middle and declining years of life there are two facts well-worth recording about our present day and age. First, the life-span has gone up to seventy or more from about forty a century ago. This alone seems to account for many of our social problems such as the proportionately higher number of middle-aged and elderly people living in any large community. Some of these are non-productive. Secondly, there is a relative and absolute increase in the number of those over seventy, causing a tremendous shift in the demographic structure of contemporary society. Already in 1950 it was expected that by 1970 the population structure in the United States would have reached a critical stage inasmuch as 10% would be over seventy. The under twenty-fives and over sixty-fives together are becoming a proportionately larger section of the whole population. They are also becoming less productive, the younger because of education, the older because of retirement policies. These factors are reflected in the religious life. The thirty to sixty age-range is rapidly becoming the productive sector upon whom the rest depend.

Senescence and Senility

There is an enormous difference between senescence and senility. Senescence is the other side of the hill corresponding to adolescence: adolescence, maturity, senescence. It is a much slower process than adolescence having a less steep slope; it is not a pathological state any more than is adolescence. The latter is a perfectly normal state of maturation, and senescence should still be looked upon as a period of further maturation. Put it this way: We could think of maturation from conception through birth, infancy, childhood, the slowing down of the latency years, the tremendous burst of the pre-pubertal period, puberty, and this going on until the slowing down at eighteen to twenty-five; at twenty-five there is a plateau and this lasts only about five to eight years; at thirty-three the senescence process sets in and is continuous from then on. Thirty-three is a critical point. Physiologically, we know that in the early thirties even the cubic capacity of the cortex begins to shrink. More to the point is this: from thirty-three onwards you find a progressive slowing down in all sorts of ways. (This age is chosen arbitrarily as senescence does not happen just like that any more than adolescence does at twelve; this is about the age it sets in.) The aspect to be stressed is not the shrinking of the cortex, nor the slowing down of the reflexes, but the fact that this is still a maturation process. Unlike other organisms man can simultaneously decline physically and progress humanly. Because we confused these two facts in the past we still tend to think of physical decline as though it were a personality decline.

Senility on the other hand is a declining process. It is not pathological, though there are pathological processes than can occur in senility. Rather this process is a real decline in power which is still compatible with personality progress, and it is only the pathological functions of senility that are incompatible with personality progress. These functions are the dementias, involutional and degenerative processes where there is a loss of rational functioning which may be accompanied by disorientation in space and time, entry into a fantasy-world, pathological guilt-feelings, and warped judgment. Apart from these processes, even senility ought to be years of progress from the personality viewpoint.

One can date the senescence process from the early thirties, but one does not expect senility to commence until the late sixties, early seventies or much later. Very frequently it will be only in the eighties before these processes are manifested and then only under certain conditions. For instance, if you hospitalize a person of sixty, seventy, seventy-five as a senile patient and leave it at that, then you will have a serious decline on your hands in a short time. If you employ good geriatrics, for example, setting tasks within the compass of the aging person and making demands which seem a little beyond their resources, this decline need not take place for another ten or even twenty years. The very fact of making these demands and expecting them to be met makes an individual feel wanted and again offsets the involutional or declining process.

The Under-Thirty Generation

Let us look back to the thirties. There are certain definable changes here. These occur first on the level of the cognitive and skilled processes and then on the level of the emotional and personality processes. There is a slight increase of intelligence between the ages of fifteen and twenty-five. Usually, fifteen to sixteen can be taken as the period of maximal expansion. In terms of functioning in our type of society we can even concede a slight increase up to twenty-five years, but from then on to about fifty-five there is no significant increase. To put it another way, intelligence remains more or less constant. Nevertheless, even as early as thirty-three other changes appear, not in intellectual capacity but in the functioning of the whole person with regard to the cognitive and skilled processes. If you read the biographies of the great mathematicians, the really great ones who made the breakthroughs, you will find that if a man has not made his great discovery before twenty-five, he never makes it. The greatest original discoveries were made by them in their early twenties. Einstein made his great breakthrough in the theory of relativity before he was twenty-five, and it was another eleven years before he arrived at the general theory. Descartes made his breakthrough in co-ordinate geometry by the age of twenty-two. George Boole was publishing his new Boolean algebra at nineteen. Lobeczewcky was working out his fourth dimensional geometry at twenty-three.

All this means that a special kind of intelligence related to the highest function of the intellect is at its best at this early age. We must not allow this fact to dull our perception. While the great breakthrough is made before twenty-five, perhaps the most valuable work is done later on, namely, the development of the great "insight," the proving of its truthfulness and the working out of its implications.

The change in the intellectual performance from twenty-five onwards is a change in quality which can best be thought of as a penetration in depth rather than the flash of insight of the pre-twenty-five period. We expect the young person in college or university to have the brilliant flash of insight, but we forget that the real operation of the discursive reason is not the brilliant flash of insight but the penetration in depth over time. And so what happens is this: we lead the young person to the flash of insight; he gets his degree, and from then on he teaches elementary algebra or routine texts of history. There is no further penetration in depth where this is precisely the quality of his intelligence at this time. We allow him to go fallow as he reads magazines, etc. It would be fairly interesting to do a survey of the reading habits of the gifted graduates in your communities. It would show up one of the major flaws in our current ways of forming persons.

It has been said that because of this change of gear from the flash of insight to the penetration in depth that it is impossible to form a new idea when you are over forty. This is very true. It is very easy to acquire a new verbal skill, to learn to make the right answers, as it was easy to do this in the four- to seven-year-old age group. You can teach a child of five to define a triangle for you or to give you the formula: $E = mc^2$, but you cannot argue from that that he knows physics or has learned the theory of relativity. After forty, something similar takes place. We learn to say all the right things, but it is awfully difficult to form the corresponding idea. This must be borne in mind because this is the basic difficulty of the post-conciliar world. The young people can see clearly because of the flash of insight which is their quality of intelligence and they can conceptualize. We older ones try penetration in depth, learning the words, and some of good-will live by the words they have learned but very few can in fact form the corresponding concepts. Does this mean we must despair? No. But it means we have to be ready to be guided by youngsters whose flash of insight is so often enormously illuminating.

Skills

The most striking change in the middle years is not in the intellectual field. It is in the field of skilled performance, skill here meaning the carrying out of any learned activity which is adaptive to changing stimuli. Routine activity is not skill in this terminology. If a sister has learned to bake a particular kind of cake and does this for every "feast day," this is not skill. It is a routine re-instatement of a concatenated set of learned patterns of behavior; skill is the capacity to adapt a learned pattern of behavior to a set of changing circumstances. Again, a teacher who has learned to teach catechism or arithmetic in a particular method can do this for the rest of his/her life. This is not skill but the re-instatement of a chain reaction. Skilled teachers are those who can adapt what they are doing to the reality they discover in the classroom, to the demands of society, to changing text books. You will find many complaining: "Why couldn't we stick to the old catechism? What is the point of all these illustrations? Why all these visual aids? Why don't they learn their religion as we did?" All this illustrates a refusal to adapt one's acquired ability in a skill to changing circumstances. This is typical of the generation of the thirty-year-olds and over. This group is actually given a certain security; it is reinforced in its conviction of its own righteousness by the fact that it refuses to adapt its skilled processes to change. The skill has been turned into a routine stereotype piece of behavior. This change in skills can be illustrated perhaps in various ways.

Skilled performance differs mostly from stereotyped re-instatement of unchanged patterns inasmuch as it involves the interpretation of the new incoming stimuli. A simple example is the skilled action of a person playing tennis or cricket. He has to watch the stimulus and adapt the most complicated co-ordination of muscular ability in response to a stimulus approaching at fifty or sixty miles per hour, barely at the threshold of visibility. If he can do that he is a skilled performer. The stimulus comes and is received at the periphery of the organism. The response is made by the organism, however we forget to wonder what happens in between. In the case of a non-skilled response very little goes on in between, but in a skilled operation what happens is that the incoming stimulus is instantly translated into the appropriate response. With better instrumentation and greater insight in studying these things, we find that the real change in the middle-age group is not in the receptor system. It is not that your retina or the rods and cones in the retina are slower to respond to the stimulus, nor that the passage along the optic-nerve fibres is slower; neither is it that the movement from the cortex to the periphery is slower. You do not take longer to send out a signal to put out your hand to the left or the right. The delay is not here and it certainly is not along the observable, peripheral activity. You can make a gesture at thirty-three as fast as you can at twenty-five or forty-five depending on the kind of skill the act requires. The real problem comes in the translation process occurring in the cortex, the translation of the stimulus into the response, or the translation of a stimulus in one modality into a response in another. To carry out a manual response to an auditory stimulus involves a translation process. Here is where the slowing-down process takes place in senescent functions. This accounts for the fact that the speed of reaction or the apparent immediacy of the skilled response of the thirty-three-year-old is less perfect than that of the twenty-five-year-old. At the same time, this very translation process and its slowing-down may ensure a much higher accuracy in the eventual response. An industry may have to pay for its middle-aged worker by accepting the slowing-down of the assembly line, but it may gain greatly from this worker by fewer faulty end-products.

This can be translated into roles in the religious life and it is worth thinking about the skills and demands we make on persons. Perhaps our thinking has been colored by the fact that we tended to relate age-levels to certain types of work and as a result a stereotyped structure has arisen in communities where one may feel reluctant to send older people for specialized training. This is based on the fact that we did not understand the change occurring and thought incorrectly that a person at thirty-five was unable to learn a language as well as a person of fifteen, or that one at forty-five obviously was unfit to be trained as a psychologist. On the contrary, people can function quite efficiently in a new intellectual field at forty-five and over.

Emotional Life

Another plane that must be considered is that of the emotional, affective life. The changes on the emotional, affective side are far more important than those concerning the intellectual life because they are more universal and perhaps more distressing. From about thirty-three onwards, in a woman's case, there is an awareness of a decline in the physical dimensions of personality. In a man's case this does not begin to operate until closer to forty-five. Secondly, there occurs a loss of appetite for things which seemed to be intensely enjoyable up to the age of thirty-three to thirty-five. This goes for both men and women. There is a loss of keenness, of the expected intensity of response. Perhaps for most people this is not a problem, but for some it is agonizing. They discover that what had primacy in their affective life no longer attracts. The layperson at this age level will say: "I just don't enjoy movies any more. I haven't danced for years. Television is a waste of time. I can't even read a book." What are they describing? The awareness of the decline in the piquancy of life, the awareness of the fact that they have set certain kinds of experience as goals, and these are failing them and there is a general slump experienced. In the religious life the same thing takes place. Things that seemed to be peak events, making weeks of drudgery tolerable, no longer operate. Or to change the metaphor, the lubricants are now a source of friction. The celebration of Mother Provincial's feast day, which was a day of joy and exhilaration when you were a novice, has now become a routine business. This has to be looked at carefully. I am using this example only as a symbol. You can spread it right across the whole range of your daily activities and wonder whether we have made any attempt to meet the genuine needs of persons in age-brackets.

"How weary, stale, flat, and unprofitable seem to me all the uses of the world!" This phrase ought to be carved over the doors of all religious houses throughout the whole structure of the Church. Then religious would become accustomed to the concept as being a perfectly normal, ordinary dimension of life. What happens is that when religious reach this stage, they read it instead to mean: "How weary, stale, flat, and unprofitable seem to me all the uses of the

religious life! Why did I ever start?" They are reading it
in the wrong dimension. They say: "There must be something wrong with me because I feel this way about things."
But they should have been told from the beginning that they
will reach a plateau where the only meaningful statement
they will be able to make is: "How weary, flat, stale, and
unprofitable is all this whole business!" At that stage you
will have learned that the dimension of experience is totally
irrelevant. This is where the non-experiential motivations
have to be drawn on, those motivations we call faith and
grace.

The first manifestation of a genuine emotional change
is this awareness of futility. This is perfectly normal; there
is nothing pathological about it. We are not speaking here
of people on the decline but about a facet of maturation.
We can even state it is a sign of continuing maturation that
one should realize how futile is most of what one is doing.
This is good Pauline teaching, and, indeed, it is good
Scripture teaching: "When you have done all these things,
say, we are unprofitable servants" (Lk 17:10). This beginning of the experience of futility, failure, etc., is the point
which is now coming to be called the "awakening" by contemporary psychiatrists. The study of these things is part
of a world-wide process at present, one of the insights
emerging being that this experience is a normal stimulus
for the organism to turn round and face itself once again
to take the next step forward. Instead of reading it as a
failure or breakdown, one should begin to read it as a productive, emotional disintegration, just as the tantrums of
the four-year-old and the conflicts of the adolescent are not
to be read as pathological but as productive, emotional dis-

integrations. This awakening and confrontation are often read by one going through them as: "This is the time for me to get some fresh carpet-slippers, a few more privileges, and sit back and do nothing."

Just as there is the typical "malaise" of the adolescent, so also there is the typical anxiety of the middle-age group. This anxiety is a diffused awareness that suffuses one's being just below the threshold of consciousness, but at almost any moment it can break through, especially if the stimulus is applied which would make a person feel anxious. In this case the anxiety now released will be out of all proportion to the stimulus. Again, a stimulus which may not be expected to produce anxiety may do so in a flood. If mother superior says to a sister of thirty-five or forty: "Pull yourself together and we will send you to convent X," sister gets terribly anxious. Her anxiety verbalized is: "The superior does not like me. I know the mistress of novices didn't want me here. Maybe I am not where I ought to be. I should never have started." In a man, anxiety, again running under the surface, appears early in the forties and he learns quickly to handle it with a little alcohol. We should think very carefully about the different kinds of motivation leading to alcohol, drug-taking, hypochondria.

Fear of Death

All this anxiety is linked with the deepest of all the dynamisms activating the human psyche, the fear of death. At each stage of the developmental process there is a typical fear, not a learned fear but an endogenous fear stemming from our finite state. These are not incidental to human life, but are as constitutive of human life as are food and drink and maternal affection. The first fear is the fear of the unknown in infancy and childhood. The child of two knows nothing about what bathing in the sea is like, so he is automatically frightened of the sea. His mother has to teach him not to be afraid. This goes for all sorts of other areas. The second fear appears in adolescence and consists in being overcome by the forces of our unconscious, the fear of the depths of my "self." This is the reason for the search for identity at this time. It is the reassurance that I can handle my anger, my instinctual drives and desires. I am not going to be overcome by fear. If the adolescent gets the idea he cannot handle these things, he will express it this way: "I think I am going crazy!"

The fear of death is not typical of either childhood or adolescence. This fear emerges after the twenty-five to thirty-three plateau. It is a wholly inescapable fear. It can be ignored up to the thirties as long as the individual is still in progress up the line of maturation. It can be ignored as long as there are sufficient stimuli engaging the whole person's outward-regarding attention. Withdraw those and the turn inwards begins and the fear appears. The whole point of this fear is that it should be a launching-pad for reappraisal. It is also possible to deny this as some women do in middle age. The woman does not say she does not fear death, but she will say: "I can still dance as well as my daughter. I can still enjoy parties." The man will say: "Who is worried about coronaries? I am still going to enjoy golf and tennis every day." This is another way of saying: "I am not going to allow this fear of death to emerge."

Problems of Old Age

We can summarize in a series of propositions the main factors regarding the middle years. The first is the clash of generations A, B, C. The A-generation is the grandparents; the B-generation is the parents; and the C-generation is the children. The analogues hold in the religious life: A equals the power-holding seniors, B equals the ten to twenty years professed who have no real power to operate; and C equals the so-called "young professed" who may indeed be quite old in chronological age. They may already be over the hump of complete maturation in the twenty-five to thirty age-group and already in the declining years. However they are still "young" in the eyes of the two other generations.

Secondly, adapting what the geriatric people tell us about the growing old process, we should carry out a survey within any group to discover who is doing what and why. This means a job-analysis and an attempt to relate the findings to the resources of the people. It is time we began to wonder about the waste of potential in our priestly and religious houses. Those of us who are in charge of forming people will have to "render an account" not just for the souls but the talents of our subjects. The members of the community will not be answerable for burying the talent because they could not do otherwise, but the superior who makes them do it will have to answer for it. This loss of potential is enormous. In fact, if we got a management-consultant group to do a study of any large-scale Congregation or of the diocesan clergy the loss of potential they would discover would be frightening. The most alarming dimension of this is the fact that we all settle for a happy, comfortable mediocrity because things run more smoothly that way. The loss is not just that of one's individual potential, but a drop in the total functioning of society.

The two next points are obvious. One is the jealousy appearing in the B-generation with regard to the privileges and opportunities of the C-generation. Part of the problem arises because the former has not been prepared for the cultural revolution taking place in which these privileges and opportunities are normal. For example, it is now normal for a secondary school product to go on for university education. It is normal and when this cannot be done it is extraordinary. The B-generation does not realize this. It still thinks of these things as rather extraordinary. "We do it because of the apostolate" or: "The Superior General says we must and the Council insists and so we must send everyone out for training." The younger members will enjoy their time in training and why not? This is intrinsic to the process they are going through. They have a great deal of liberty and this is as it ought to be. Instead of regarding this as a loss, it should be looked upon as a gain in personality structure.

The other point is this: in the middle years there is a decline in one's clarity of vision. This decline is a decline in the clarity of intellectual vision to things and they lose their clarity and we do not see them any more. All the formulae given and activated through the twenties and thirties lose their meaning. This sudden drop in clarity of vision is one of the things we have to watch carefully and prepare for by making a clear distinction between the felt-dimensions and the non-perceptible dimensions of our lives.

Hypochondria is the real danger for priests and brothers

of this age-group. I am not sure about sisters. A good deal of the symptomatology is due, for example, to faulty ways of living, bad diet, too little exercise, too many pills, and too much concentration on an infantile type of self-regard. All these things should be looked at very carefully because they are all part of the personality processes.

Finally, we must remember that constant, long-range preparation for these years ought to be as much a part of our thinking as the preparation of the child for adolescence and the adolescent for adulthood.

PART III: THE THREE VOWS

10. AN OVERVIEW

In the human being the living organism is the person. Not all persons are living organisms, nor are all living organisms persons. Thus the three divine Persons are not living organisms; angels are persons but not organisms; there are many species of organisms in existence, none are persons except man. He is unique in being a living organism and a person. He does not automatically grow into what he ought to be, for he has to be formed. This formation involves an adequate biological endowment called the genes to ensure normal maturation. Secondly, the person is formed by the actions he carries out as we become what we do, we make ourselves by our choices. Thirdly, we need things. The three vows are not to be regarded as separate entities but as a continuum. They are not selected arbitrarily but are necessary if the religious is to be totally consecrated. They form a continuum by which the living organism, the actions it performs, and the things it needs are all consecrated. Thus the three vows are one's way of expressing total consecration, the means of converting the potential creature into the perfect man.

Chastity

The vow of chastity must be seen as a positive consecration of the living organism or person. It should be seen
primarily as a sign of consecration. Obviously this consecration will be and will become sacrificial, however this
is a consequence of the vow and not its essence. Since the
Incarnation there can be no question about the value of
human nature and the transcendental value of being a
person. This is part of the Christian revelation, and it is in
the mystery of the Incarnation and in the value of the person that we find the beginning of the theology of chastity.
Instead of looking upon this vow in the form of "thou shalt
not" or "thou shalt," we should think of it as a single facet
of the value of being a person which is the radical revelation of the Incarnation. This mystery was the revelation of
a Person, not a human person but a Person with a complete
human nature. Personality with a capital "P" was revealed.
And chastity is a dimension of that. Let us forget the negative
approach to this virtue and take the positive one of: "Thou
shalt be an inviolable person."

We are not concerned here in this concept with the
relatively few who have never sullied their baptismal in-
nocence, but with persons who are now inviolate, whose
integrity as persons has been restored if it was ever lost,
and who now consecrate the living body as part of the
restoration of all things in Christ. Sacramental absolution
means a restoration to the status in which we were. It does
not mean that we are left scarred nor that our sins are simply
covered over or ignored by God. Only God can annihilate
as only he can create. When we are absolved from sin, our
sin is taken out of time and history as though it had never

been. This should be stressed more because of the confusion in many minds between physical virginity and the practice of chastity. Physical virginity is not the same as the inviolate personality who chooses chastity. A child's physical virginity is not the same as the adult's consecrated chastity. The stress laid sometimes on the notion of physical virginity has made the life of consecrated chastity seem to some as unattainable. We should explain more fully to young people that the obligations of chastity are part of their perfecting as persons, part of their growth, part of their becoming inviolate persons. This is important in order to counteract present teachings. Young people are being led to believe that the life-long observance of chastity means in some way that they are not being fulfilled as persons, as though the fulfilling of biological generation were intrinsic to one's fulfillment as a person. And some think that once physical virginity is lost they can never become consecrated virgins. This is a mistake.

For the perfecting of the Christian called to the life of perfection sexual fulfillment may be both indispensable and intrinsic to his vocation. Chastity, however, is still an essential part of his vocation, though he is not called upon to take the vow of chastity. We should remind ourselves that the title of the late Pius XI's encyclical on marriage was "Chaste Wedlock." In other words, Christians called to perfection in the world are called upon to observe chastity in marriage. One interesting facet here is that chastity and the appropriate fulfillment of the sexual function are not incompatible. Although the human person and the living organism are one and the same, nevertheless the person's fulfillment lies not in the fulfillment of the organism as such, but in the fulfilling of the precise function in virtue of which we are persons.

This function is not the biological one we share with other organisms, but the rational function of reasoning and willing by which we are distinct from them.

The world cannot understand chastity nor the consecrated virgin. In its eyes chastity is a lack of fulfillment, a stunting of growth, a lopping off of something of our personality. We understand it better if we ask: "Does God lack something by not fulfilling this function? Do the angels?" The answer is no. We share our peculiar privilege with God. Paternity (and maternity) in this world are called after the paternity of God the Father. "For this reason I bow my knees before the Father from whom every family in heaven and earth is named...." (Eph 3:14-15). God's fatherhood is a non-biological generation. All generation is in some degree a sharing of God's creativity, however we are the only creatures capable of non-biological reproduction. We have the capacity to reproduce ourselves in other ways. The words we use show that we are aware of an affinity between biological and non-biological reproduction, for example, one conceives a child but one also conceives a thought or an idea. The artist, the novelist, the sculptor reproduce themselves in their works. These are specifically human creativities in which no other creatures can share. This is a kind of reproduction and fulfillment which is ours in the practice of virginity and celibacy.

Obedience

Obedience is a moral relationship between persons. To make a vow of obedience means that every act of every area of one's life is consecrated. Just as the organism itself is consecrated through chastity, and the extension of the personality into things is consecrated through poverty, so also the whole range of behavior is consecrated through obedience. We have tended under pressure from legal forms of thinking to limit obedience to such matters as would be thought as binding gravely in conscience. This is a mistake. Undoubtedly, there are limits and legal aspects of this vow which must be carefully considered. These are not, however, the essence of the vow. They form part of the complex framework of interpersonal relationships, sometimes governed by legal or moral sanctions constituting the complex social structure of the religious life. But the true meaning, the essence of the vow do not lie in those aspects, but rather in the totality of the person's consecration. As long as the individual is in any sense doing whatever is appropriate to his role at the moment, he is living his vow of obedience. It is only when one is doing what one ought not to be doing that there is a violation. Even when an action is totally optional and it appears as though the person is making a choice in his own right, his act is consecrated through the vow. Obedience is not a depersonalizing of oneself, not a way of "submitting the will" to another, not a legal device to be interpreted minimally. It is the consecration of all the events that make a person the kind of person he is.

Poverty

Man's organic growth, governed by genetic endowment, needs an appropriate environment in which to develop. He has to choose and form his own environment. Ownership of property is one aspect of this relationship between man and his environment. It is a moral relationship established between him and things. For the perfecting of man in the natural order some form of this relationship is normally in-dispensable. It involves a mine-thine distinction and some form of this distinction is necessary for growth in the natural order. All that is needed is the instrumental use of things and what happens in the religious life is that we revert to the purely instrumental use of things.

Property is an extension of the personality into things. That is why there is a natural right to property. It is a natural right because many are so inadequate as persons that their growth depends on things. If a person is so inadequate that his growth depends on things, one can see how very mature one must be before he can dispense with this relation-ship. Thus poverty becomes a prerogative of very mature persons who feel no need to extend their personality into things. They have reached a stage where they are complete within themselves, having no need of the space-time co-or-dinates to tell them who or what they are.

In its document on the Religious Life, Vatican II states: "Let religious painstakingly cultivate poverty and give it new expressions if need be" (par. 13). This requires some understanding of the cultural dimensions of property and wealth. The old ways of practicing poverty were based on the old ways of owning property. And the old ways of owning property were based on the concept of personal ownership of objects called private property. Poverty as conceived in the West and in religious life has been re-lated exclusively to the notion of individual persons holding outright certain kinds of property. Both feudal and capitalistic societies were rooted in this concept, although the numbers of people owning property in this way varied a great deal between the two societies. It was perhaps easy to express poverty in either type of society by identification with the destitute, the dispossessed, the poverty-stricken. We must try to understand the question of new dimensions or expressions of poverty by asking what other forms of ownership there can be.

This becomes clear if we look at a society where not only does the individual not own property, except for the bare essentials, but where even the collectivity cannot own capital. How would religious as individuals or as a religious society express poverty in Rumania or Russia today? In a socialized democracy such as the welfare state of Great Britain the problem is different. Where every citizen is in theory to be cared for throughout life as a matter of legal right, ownership in the old sense is rendered redundant, and not to own property oneself is not the definition of poverty. This is one way of seeing that the concept of poverty has to change as the concept of property changes. New ways of understanding poverty in our culture might be allied to an understanding of the notion of "credit-worthiness" in our time. Credit is the new way of property. To be worthy of credit is far more valuable than having money in the bank. The measure of one's status in contemporary society might very well be the measure of one's credit-worthiness. It would seem that in this regard religious are in danger of being regarded as wealthy. This is not said as a reproach. It is put forward as a basis for attempting some form of breakthrough which has not as yet been made. The real essence of poverty might be found to lie in the renunciation of collective credit-worthiness, and not simply in not owning a silver pencil or in not having a transistor in one's room.

With reference to the individual and poverty we may have confused poverty with its outward signs. We have thought that if we did not appear to have anything then **we** are poor. We have thought that if one has to transport himself from A to B, then one should get a second-hand car instead of a new car. Poverty entails the absence of the moral relationship to things, but it still enjoins the things necessary for perfecting of the personality. And this in turn enjoins the things necessary for the proper fulfillment of one's professional role. The perfecting of the personality must be seen in terms of role and professional status. Not owning things which is not the same as poverty must not be allowed to interfere with what is necessary either to personal growth or to role fulfillment. It is important to have all the equipment conducive to the adequate fulfillment of a rule, whether as a student, teacher, or member of any profession. As our social conscience develops and as state agencies take more and more care of the citizens, poverty in the sense of destitution has diminished. This is not to say that there are not destitute people and sometimes great poverty. It is to state that our social conscience is at least alive to this and efforts are made to deal with it. The real poor in our type of society are the modestly well-educated, white-collar workers who are perpetually struggling to pay off a mortgage, never able to reach a comfortable bank balance, unable to provide for the future, and always slightly behind in the inflationary cycle. Perhaps this might be a useful model for religious poverty today.

One of the difficulties in the matter of behavior is the distinction between the absence of a particular act and the positive possession of a particular virtue. A virtue is an acquired disposition inclining one to behave in a particular way. The fundamental problem about chastity is this: in what does the virtue of chastity consist? It cannot lie simply in the absence of unchaste acts as a virtue cannot be simply a negation.

Chastity — A Form of Loving

Chastity is a form of loving. If we ask what sort of loving it is, it is difficult to answer. It is the virtue which inclines one person to love another without seeking gratification from or possession of the loved person. The absence of these two factors is at least part of the specification of chastity as a way of loving. An infant's loving is strictly possessive. The infant rivals the father for the mother's affection, becoming envious because he wants to possess her outright. The adolescent's loving is self-gratifying. Even what appears to be a romantic, idealized, detached sort of loving is still self-gratifying. The adolescent boy sees himself reflected in the girl he thinks he loves and vice versa. This is why it does not last. This is why the possibility of success in marriage is related inversely to the age at which the couple enters marriage between the ages of sixteen and twenty-five. If one enters marriage in the late teens or early twenties, the chance of a happy marriage increases as the ages go up and decreases as they go down, for in the early ages a boy or girl loves with a self-gratifying love. Now when we grow into adulthood we do not shed the child or adolescent we were because we cannot. We shall find that our loving is still to some extent possessive and self-gratifying. The adult must proceed to a third dimension of loving and this is giving without seeking a recompense. One might describe the loving that is chastity as the capacity to accept another person totally, without possession, without evaluation. This is a translation of the law of charity—love your neighbor as yourself.

So this is a special kind of loving. Notice that this acceptance of the other person does not exclude affection, but neither is it specified by affection. In other words, felt-states of human affection are not intrinsic to this sort of loving but they are not excluded by it. The best way one might convey its nature is by a kind of symbolic gesture— the extended arms of Pope John as he embraced the whole world. One accepts the other person totally as one would accept a child, and just as we would not seek to possess the child exclusively nor receive one child to the exclusion of another, so one does not seek to possess exclusively in chaste loving.

In the thinking of many the idea is rampant that one can acquire the virtue of chastity only through exposure to its opposite. This is an ancient tradition. Milton has it that one must go through vice to acquire virtue. If one remembers that both Christ and Mary were perfect in their form of loving others, one can easily see that this view is wrong. With reference to those who wish to make a vow of chastity in the religious life it is asked: "Is it right to allow young people to take such a vow at the age of twenty-one or so without having experienced the world? Do they know what they are doing?" It is important that they should be mature, but we should not confuse this with having been exposed to a sexual relationship.

The Vow and Virtue of Chastity

If one asks what sort of acts must one carry out to acquire this virtue, the answer is very difficult. We hear, for instance, that one should say one's prayers, but this is not acquiring the virtue though it may be a pre-requisite to its acquisition. We should first make a distinction between the vow and the virtue. We can, by one act, impose the vow on ourselves, but we cannot acquire the virtue this way. The virtue is a special kind of loving and hence is acquired by repeated acts of this kind of loving. It is not a state one enters but a condition of behavior. The importance of this is that whereas as one takes the vow of chastity, nevertheless the virtue must be renewed choosing, a renewed choosing over and over again. This has to be said because young religious, both male and female, have their confidence badly shaken when they wake up some morning to find the strongest urge to leave the virginal state. The first question to ask such a one is how often he/she has renewed their choice of this state? If the answer is once a year, every retreat, etc., this is not enough. The renewed choosing must be carried out daily and possibly even constantly.

Eternal Generation of the Son

What is the theological basis of chastity? In St. Paul's view of God and the world all paternity in the world is named after God's paternity (cf. Eph 3:14). God's fatherhood is the primary fatherhood and the generation of the Son is the primary generation. All fatherhood, and we can link it with all motherhood, is called or becomes real as a reflection of the divine fatherhood. The same may be said for all generation which is a reflection of the eternal generation of the Son. In other words, biological reproduction is a shadow reflecting in some aspects the eternal generation in the Trinity. Hence we can say: chastity lies in the Holy Spirit, in the kind of love resulting from the eternal generation of the Son by the Father. This is the ultimate theological source. It is that kind of loving. In an eternal generation the Father begets the Son in his own image and in the eternal begetting of the Son this wholly real loving becomes another Person. We cannot imitate that. What we can remember is that the kind of loving involved in human generation is a pale shadow of the reality of the eternal generation of the Son.

The Generation of the New Creature in Baptism

The next step is a little difficult. We know that the Christian being is the only living creature who reproduces himself without biological reproduction. And that is not metaphor. St. Paul speaks of "begetting in the gospel" and he speaks of the new life in the sacrament of baptism where again he is not speaking metaphorically. This is really a new coming-to-be. The creature after baptism is a new creature in the sense that whereas all the visible dimensions are the same the whole reality is different. The creature which existed with a purely natural, generated existence now exists with a supernatural created existence. This transformation is equivalent to the generation of a new creature and this is what St. Paul calls it. No organism other than man is capable of a non-biological reproduction. Think of chastity as a loving which is specific to our human state, our state of being capable of generation and reproduction in a non-biological way and without possession of the object loved.

The Incarnation

The third theological base is the Incarnation itself. If we do not see chastity in the light of the Incarnation, we have missed altogether what it means. In a strictly theological sense the Incarnation is the source of this new life in Christ begun at our baptism. The Incarnation is the source of that new life whereby from now on human nature must live the life of grace. We forget most of the time that this life of grace is a new life in the most literal sense. One must cease to think of grace as a kind of force added to the living organism or of thinking of it in the metaphor we have used for so long, namely that of "washing clean the stain of sin." We must cease to think of it even as an addition to the person, body and soul, here and now existing. It is not that. It is a substantial transformation of the person here and now existing. It is a change in his mode of being. His very existence is altered. So after the Incarnation and because of the grace of Christ, the very flesh lives by grace. That is its existence. We have not two existences, although we have thought we had. We have thought of ourselves living with a temporal existence which remains unchanged while grace is added and grace removed. It is not like that at all. One has not a temporal existence to which grace is added. The reality is that the very existence of the organism itself is transformed by grace. We are a new creature. Even in this world grace is eternal life, not just its pledge. "This is eternal life that they may know thee, the one true God, and Jesus Christ whom thou hast sent" (Jn 17:3).

The Incarnation is the basis of all this. Christ is the Son of God. But if we ask, "How is he God?" theologians will help us to see how this might be so. His human nature is complete, but human nature complete in itself does not necessarily mean a human existence. That is why the existence can be of different orders while human nature remains the same. Christ's human nature is not a complete person, but Christ himself is a complete person. His humanity exists by the divine existence and this is exactly the same as the divinity itself, God's essence and existence being one. So human nature exists by the divine existence in Christ; human nature exists by human existence in you and me. But this human existence that we have by nature is replaced in the new begetting in the gospel. In the new generation through baptism we have also received a divine existence. In us this is a participated divine existence, whereas in Christ it is the whole, real, complete, divine existence in all its substantial reality. Our participated divine existence is what we call grace. The very flesh is transformed in its very existence and in its innermost reality though not in any observable dimension. That is where chastity lies and this becomes important when we add to it a philosophical concept which is vital to the whole theme.

The Living Flesh

In Christian revelation we do not just believe in the soul's immortality but also in the resurrection of the body. This again is a result of the Incarnation. Our body will be glorified which is another transformed existence. Why should the body share in eternal life? The answer is: "You are not a soul but a living organism." We tended to think that we were body and soul but primarily soul and that the soul dwells in the prison-house of the flesh, seeking release to return to heaven its true home. We should say in the most literal sense: "I am the living flesh and not something dwelling in this body. I am the living body." The mystery for Christianity is not how the soul is united to the body, but how the soul could ever be released from the body and what sort of being it is when released. When released it is not a complete person; it is not myself, but part of what I was. We are specified by our body.

It is vital for the development of the right attitude to chastity to recognize that one is the body. Spiritual writing in the past (and we still hear echoes of it today) seemed to be teaching that chastity consisted somehow in a "getting away from the body," in a denial or a repudiation. Virtue cannot consist in any distortion of the truth. This denial or repudiation is another word for "self-control." You are the living body or the "self" that exercises this control. This "self" is not a disembodied spirit hovering round the cortex and manipulating your limbs on strings like a puppet. It is identical with the three-dimensional, living body. And chastity lies in my attitude toward this living body. A violation of chastity is not my will or my soul doing something to the body, but the body behaving in a particular way.

There is one further step to be taken in this matter. St. Paul speaks of the body as being the "living temple of the Holy Spirit" (1 Cor 6:19). It is difficult to explain how this can be. We speak of the soul and the "indwelling of the Trinity" in the soul, and "infused grace" as inhering in the soul. St. Paul is not speaking in philosophical terms but stating a most literal truth which he frequently repeats. Since we are the living flesh and the Holy Spirit dwells in this flesh, there is a basis for reverence for the body. We reverence the body by respecting the person who is the living flesh redeemed by Christ and in whom the Spirit dwells. It is important to read the whole of chapter 15 of St. Paul's first letter to the Corinthians.

Chastity — A Way of Being Human

These notions are the basic, theological source of all teaching about this virtue. To speak of chastity as a virtue in isolation is very misleading. It is not acquired by the will operating in a vacuum. Chastity is a way of being human. Instead of speaking of an abstraction called "chastity," to speak about a reality called a "chaste person" is more appropriate. This reality involves you and me in our entirety and chastity is meaningless when isolated from the rest of our personality. Far too many people believe it is possible to be chaste while leaving other appetites to take care of themselves. Let us talk about the "chaste person."

A "chaste person" is one who has acquired a very high level of mastery over all his emotions, appetites and desires. We have seen that chastity resides in the whole living flesh. This mastery of the emotions, appetites and desires is never totally realized. We are not trying to set up impossible ideals or principles which are self-defeating, but a considerable level of self mastery is possible. Chastity cannot be maintained in a personality where any one of the passions is out of control, where anger rules, or selfishness, hatred, etc.

Secondly, since we are speaking about a chaste person and not about a virtue in isolation or an abstraction called "chastity," let us state another principle: Chastity requires great skill in handling oneself and one's interpersonal relations. The chaste person is a very mature person. It could be said further that the immature personality may have acquired the negative side of this virtue, but not its positive aspects. Just as the infant is chaste in the sense that it cannot commit sins against chastity but has not as yet acquired the virtue, so the immature person is only on the way to chastity. This virtue requires learning, skill, and practice, and it is to be acquired only in maturity.

Thirdly, the "chaste person" who has this virtue is very honest. This honesty is not something to be contrasted with deliberate self-deception. It is honesty stemming from self-knowledge in contrast with the defenses most of us use from time to time to hide our real self from ourselves. There are the rationalizations we tend to use, the attitudes towards sexuality one finds in so many of the young and even in adults. These attitudes are expressed in such questions as: "How far can I go in this matter?" This is a dishonesty that has to be faced. We cannot measure the gravity of sin by a stop-watch. If we begin thinking this way, we are thinking in a dishonest way in the sense we are using the term dishonest here. It is a shying away from reality, a hiding, a defence. The "chaste person" is completely honest, acknowledging his own sexuality without denying, excusing, or rationalizing it. He says that being human means being a sexual creature. We can, of course, acknowledge that and still hide other aspects from ourselves of what we mean by this, for example, hide from ourselves the sexual quality of some kinds of attitudes or acts or dimensions of felt-states of affection. Or we can hide from ourselves the sexual quality of some kinds of interest or dimensions of experience. This is dishonesty. It is not a deliberate deceiving or lying but it is simply not being completely frank with oneself.

There is another way in which the "chaste person" differs a little from the one who is being slightly dishonest about this. The slightly dishonest person will get hold of a phrase which is very often true in some dimensions and extends it into other dimensions without admitting it. Let us take two examples. In current literature we read statements such as: "Every man needs to love and be loved." Fine, this is true. But the problem is: What does it mean? If we say it means felt-states of affection given and returned, then we are being dishonest with ourselves. We are not reading it for the truth that it is. The other example that comes to mind is the recurring term of "self-fulfillment." We all need this, but again the question is: Which self? The infant that I was? The adolescent that I still am? The self that I would like to be, the ideal self? Or the self that I ought to be? Which of these am I going to fulfill?

12. PSYCHOSEXUAL DEVELOPMENT

If man were merely an animal his sexual life would be nothing but mating behavior. Unfortunately, that is how sexuality is being presented to many of our young people today. It is related to procreation; however, it is not in itself simply the mating, procreative behavior of a particular kind of species. This becomes important in relation to other problems currently in the air, such as procreation and marriage, artificial control of fertility. Why is human sexuality more than mere mating behavior? There are certain uniquely specifying factors surrounding it which must not be forgotten. These are the elements of choice, symbolic behavior and sacredness, and finality.

A Sacred Choice

Men and women exercise a choice in this matter of sexuality where other organisms do not. In other words, it is a rational process. Sexuality belongs to the area of conduct and not just to that of behavior. Everything the living organism does or can do may be subsumed under the concept of behavior. The term "behavior" can be used to name each process carried out by an organism other than those processes accountable for by the fact that the organism is a physical entity in a physical world. Thus, it is subject to gravity and will fall if left unsupported in mid-air. This would hardly be considered behavior since it is a process due not to the fact that the body is an organism but a body. Within the genus "behavior" one finds a certain type of activity meriting the name of "conduct." Conduct is that section of behavior that is ego-initiated, ego-directed, ego-permitted. By behavior we mean anything the organism does merely because it is a living organism and by conduct we mean anything we do because we are persons. Human sexuality belongs to the realm of conduct. It is obvious that if a sexual process is not in the realm of conduct, for example, a reflex of the organism in sleep, such a process will not pertain to the area of moral responsibility.

Both these notions surround human sexuality in all cultures and at all times. There is no known culture which has been able to dispense with a ritual of marriage. It is inherent in man's nature that his sexuality is something sacred and this generates the need to surround it with ritual and symbol. By sacredness is meant the character of being set apart just as the religious is rendered sacred by profession or consecration. The setting apart or rendering sacred pertains not only to the virgin, but to the notion of sexuality itself. It is already set apart because it is the sexuality of a rational being, living by the life of the spirit and then, in grace, living the divine life.

Finality

The finality element is also important. Even a society which accepts easy extra-marital relationships and divorce will generally still think at least that the first marriage *ought* to be final, and that if it is not there is something amiss.

This element of finality belongs to it and any breakdown in it is somehow regarded as a violation of the sacredness of the matter. In other words, we are talking about human love and not about animal sexuality when we speak about human sexuality.

Incommunicability of Human Love

Human love eludes communicability in words. One could think, perhaps, of the whole history of man in creative literature, poetry, drama and novel, as an attempt to express and communicate the meaning of human love in terms other than itself and the attempt meets with failure because there is no way of communicating an experience in one modality, e.g., an emotion, through another medium, e.g., words. So human love is incommunicable as an experience as also are fear and anger. If one has never experienced fear, one can never know what it is. The psychologist can describe how some people behave when fearful or angry; however, he cannot tell what fear or anger is. Neither can he describe human love. It has to be experienced. The primary experience of love is that of the mother for her child, later comes the father's love, then the interpersonal relations among children, and then the wider experience of learning to love others. Human sexuality has to be seen in relation to this incommunicable dimension of human loving, not in relation to the observed behavior of organisms other than man. We have already stressed the fact that we are living organisms, the living flesh. Because we are this we must recognize that sexuality pervades our being. This does not mean that the qualitatively sexual type of experience pervades us, but that many experiences which are not sexual are nevertheless sexual processes because of the kind of creatures we are. This is part of the mystery of sexuality and chastity.

The Ordinariness of Sex

Let us consider the episode of the woman taken in adultery (Jn 7:53—8, 11). The story is familiar as is our Lord's comment: "Has no man condemned you? Neither will I condemn you. Go, and sin no more." What is the predominant note, the atmosphere? Some will say, the love of Christ, his manner of handling the Pharisees, his condescension. But perhaps the recording of this incident has another purpose. The dominant note is the complete ordinariness of the scene and the exchange between Christ and the woman. There is nothing extraordinary, nothing unusual about her condition. Not only is there an absence of rebuke and condemnation, but there is no surprise or dismay. The simple fact is that the woman is taken in adultery, our Lord sees and speaks to her accusers, and then says to her: "Has no man condemned you? . . . . Neither will I."

It is this ordinariness and its accompanying dialogue that must be noted when we read it. This is a most important, though simple, concept. We too should accept this attitude of playing-down the woman's problem. Unhappily, there has been a tradition operating for some time the other way, and it has had somewhat disastrous effects. For example, part of the ordinariness is the sheer universality of the sexual problem. Here universality means that it belongs to all normally healthy human beings. What we did in the past was to build up an attitude of fear, guilt, self-punitive feelings, repression. We managed to convey to people that it was unusual to have a problem in this matter, only bad people experienced it. What happened? People got into trouble anyway, but many experienced two reactions. First, they began to think: "What a horrible creature I am. I must be bad. I wish I were like the rest. I am beyond redemption." All this, because they had learned that this is an extraordinary thing to happen to anybody. Secondly, by regarding it as extraordinary we increased the felt-guilt about it and as a consequence people found it more difficult to accept their guilt and seek absolution. By teaching them that this was an extraordinary situation we led them to the conviction which may be expressed in these words: "Right, I am extraordinary. I am beyond the pale." This is not often put into words but this is how they feel about it. Do not misunderstand "ordinary" saying: "It is not sinful at all; it's a perfectly ordinary thing." No, it is precisely a sin, and sin in this matter is the most ordinary thing in the world, in the whole history of salvation. This means—back to our rule of loving—you must embrace all precisely because they have a problem and you must love them. This is chastity at its best, loving the person who has a real difficulty about this sort of thing.

Its Universality

Because it is such an ordinary occurrence we should not be surprised to find that the vast majority of the human race has problems in sexual behavior. In the psychologist's terminology these are called behavior problems; in the moralist's, sin. It will help if we state a few facts about this matter. We know from all the evidence that in the area of auto-erotic experience, self-stimulated sex experience or masturbation, probably 90% of all males between puberty and adulthood have a problem. We know also that most girls going through adolescence into adulthood are likely to have a problem, that certainly 50% have and very likely 75% have had a problem. It is perhaps reassuring that the person without a problem is probably an extremely privileged one in the order of grace or else he is a person who is still in a pre-adolescent stage of development. We have to choose between sanctity or immaturity to avoid any sort of problem. That is why sacrifice, self-control, and asceticism are intrinsic to virginity and chastity. It just does not happen that one escapes a problem and avoids it for long periods of time unless one is specially chosen and preserved by grace or is so immature that he or she cannot have a problem.

The final proposition regarding attitudes in sexual matters is this, we must have a healthy acknowledgment of our need for redemption. This is part of the Christian revelation. The universality of this need has as its immediate counterpart the universality of the absence of grace. If it were not for this there would be no universal need for redemption. So let us always remember that this need is predicated on sin and is directly related to the need for grace and that "where sin abounded, grace did more abound" (Rm 5:20).

Developmental Aspects

Infancy — The infant comes into the world and in the first eighteen months or so is male or female but does not have a male or female personality because it does not have a personality as yet. The child has to acquire one, learning what it is to be male or female. In these first months the child makes no distinction on a sexual basis.

Childhood — At about the age of two in our culture the child commences to recognize that boys are boys and girls are girls. He is not doing it on an organic basis but we are teaching him that boys wear one type of clothes, girls, another. Little boys get toy engines and girls get dolls. The child is also learning that he is organically different because his bathing and toilet training is somewhat different from a girl's. They are separated a little bit. Now this is a stage in which they become aware of sex differences but not precisely in sexual terms.

At three and a half to four and a half the child enters a wider world where his emotions expand in range and deepen in intensity. The child begins to experience envy, anger, anxiety, frustration. This expansion leads to a different triangle in the family where the girl rivals her mother for the father's affection and the boy, for the mother's. One of the disastrous things here is that the parents sometimes play this game, the mother refusing something and the father granting it. This creates confusion in the child. The child now begins to learn that there are hazards in getting mixed up with little girls and the girl learns the same lesson with regard to little boys. Each begins to feel insecure in the presence of the opposite sex. This leads to withdrawal to the shelter of one's own sex. This is manifested in various ways. A girl will be considered a tomboy if she seeks boys' company and wants to play their games, a boy will be considered a sissy if he does the same. So they control each other, operating a perfectly natural segregation. This has a biological function as it is a withdrawal in order to come to grips with one's internal, emotional states. Some distortions of development can occur at this time.

Why does the boy feel anxious in the girl's presence? The answer is simple. In the first two years every baby must learn about its own body and so it explores its body, putting its toe in its mouth, sucking its thumb, etc. He learns the limits of his body and in the course of the exploration he finds there is a localized and intense pleasure in the genital area. Most children will have gone through a phase of stimulating themselves, perhaps manually or by rocking or other ways. At the stage where the child emerges to play with other children this goes underground and is temporarily lost. When the child learns about the differences between the sexes, the boy becoming anxious about the girl and vice versa, this precipitates again something of the infantile process. The child is involved now with the mother and father and with all sorts of sex differences. His emotions are in turmoil. Anger, fear, desire, jealousy, love are precipitated and he withdraws for shelter in order that the emotions will go dormant again and will not disturb him.

For several years the child is comparatively tranquil, until eight or nine. During this period he will be outgoing, looking at the world and at things. Watch a boy of eight or nine at play and compare him to one at four or at ten and you will see an enormous difference. The nine-year-old will be absorbed in something other than himself, spending hours looking at a stream or trying to catch a frog or playing a game with other boys with little internal awareness, little or no turning in on himself. Whereas at four he was disturbed by his internal states and perhaps expressed this as tantrums or negativism, at ten or eleven he will express this by becoming a temporary social isolate. He may become sombre or hyper-active again as the four-year-old was and get into a state of negativism or tantrums.

During the ages of seven to nine and the withdrawal phase, the emotional problems the child must cope with are fairly straightforward. In the pre-pubertal years these can become acute, the boy being disturbed by the girl's presence and vice versa because the emotional life is undergoing a radical change, expanding in range and intensity. This phase is far more important than the actual onset of physiological puberty. For example, if a child in this pre-pubertal stage withdraws to the shelter of his/her own sex, it may be because of the fear of the expanding range of the emotional life. This fear may color his/her life from then on, for it is at this stage that one observes the emergence of the more important kinds of sexual problems affecting the individual for the future. We have mentioned the widespread problem of masturbation. Many seem to think this is only a post-pubertal problem, but one finds more and more frequently a manifestation of this same problem in the pre-pubertal years.

The explanation is this: the pre-pubertal nine to eleven phase is a re-enacting of the infantile transition. First of all one finds once again the inability to cope with internal emotional states. Tantrums which appeared at the four-year-old phase again make their appearance. Girls will throw themselves on the bed and sob and will not know how to handle their inner emotional state; boys will get violently angry. Secondly, the negativism of the child will re-emerge. The girl at school has been doing her homework, coming on time to school at six, seven, and eight years old. At nine she begins to get difficult and we say: "If they could only stay as good as they were...." The child of ten, like the child of three, is becoming aware of tremendous emotional states. She is learning more about herself in this opposition to adults; she is trying to come to grips with her instinctual life in a premature way. There is no innate knowledge of the female role or the male role, and there is no innate knowledge of how to handle instinctual life. The child has to learn to handle his/her experience of sexual shock, desire, etc. The masturbatory problem obtains here, but this is not to say that it is sinful. The child can be mishandled and led to think it is sinful, piling guilt-feelings on guilt-feelings. Or again the child may be so frightened that he/she will simply repress the whole sexual mechanism. This makes it more difficult to handle sexuality. During this period one should not think of punishing a child for this type of activity.

Puberty — There is an enormous range for the onset of puberty which can occur as early as ten. In that case the pre-pubertal stage can begin as early as seven. On the other hand, it need not occur until sixteen or seventeen. At the age of thirteen, three-quarters of all girls will have become physically mature, but it will be two years later before the same percentage of boys will have reached this stage. At fifteen about 15% of the girls will not have entered physiological maturity, so the age of onset in our type of culture varies from ten to seventeen. The result is that one cannot generalize too much about this.

A curious biological change is occurring whereby puberty is setting in on an average about four months earlier every ten years for the last one hundred and twenty years. It is a cycle that nobody understands. There will occur at some stage an advance up the scale again. It is easy to see why it is not unique if you remember that in Canon Law a girl could marry at twelve. In Eastern societies marriage at ten, eleven, and twelve is not unknown. In our type of culture what it means is this, that whereas the average age for the onset of puberty in 1840 was about sixteen for girls, it is now down to twelve and a half or twelve. This is part of the reason why there is a teenage problem and why sexuality has to be understood. Children today are said to be more honest because they are relatively more mature physiologically than we were at their age and four years more mature than their great grandparents were at the same age.

Adolescence — The post-pubertal years are the most fascinating period of human development. It is often thought that in these years the sexual problem is the most important but this is not so. The adolescent has a healthy set of defenses against sexuality. Both sexes shy away from the overtly sexual. There is a natural curiosity that goes side by side with this withdrawal. Hence the adolescent attitude is ambivalent: a shying away and an attraction. This curiosity must be acknowledged as perfectly good and desirable just as the withdrawal is natural and healthy. Because of this ambivalence the adolescent's attitude produces marked anxiety. This anxiety is far more dominant than any sexual performance or experience. Even more important the young person's real problem is not the sexual but the identity problem.

It was said earlier that the infant has to learn what it is to be a boy or girl. In the adolescent years the boy and girl have to learn their sexual roles, how one ought to behave as a boy or girl. The difference in these roles has been clouded. In the nineteenth century the sex role of the adolescent girl was simple. She learned how to become a wife and mother. The range of her skills and the demands made on her were relatively few. Similarly, with the boy the male role was relatively simple, consisting mainly in learning to leave the family unit, marrying, and then taking care of his family. In our culture learning these roles is difficult. If girls are not taught a feminine role they cannot be blamed later on if they are not very feminine.

The child goes through the adolescent years, shying away from overt sexuality and being attracted to it, confused about his/her sex role, wondering about his/her identity, and acquiring some of the skills for adulthood. Legal adulthood has been defined as twenty-one years of age. There may have been a time when this corresponded with actual adulthood, but what is happening now is that with the earlier onset of puberty and a readiness for mature procreation at thirteen or fourteen, the girl does not become adult until she is twenty-five. This means becoming adult in the sense of the adult role demanded in our society. So she has a conflict to resolve, a conflict between the demands of her mature organism and the incomplete state of her personality formation. Our society has a problem in the early onset of adolescence and the extension into the twenties of the adolescent role. Society does not demand the adult role from adolescents until twenty-three, twenty-five, or even later. This can be seen by the fact that adolescent behavior is condoned in university students, behavior that would have been punished in high school a generation ago. This type of behavior is condoned at what would be adult years because society is conceding adolescent status to the young man who can run a riot successfully. This is a problem of our culture.

Adult Desire — The rhythm of sexual demand varies between boys and girls. With boys there is usually a period in the second half of adolescence when sexual demand becomes acute; for most girls this is a relatively tranquil period but by twenty-two the girl enters a period of acute demand. One thing they are not being prepared for is precisely this kind of experience. They are prepared for the onset of puberty, but they are not prepared for the experience of desire. It is an extremely difficult thing to do. This desire is not necessarily recognized as qualitatively sexual because often it is not so. What is experienced is an undifferentiated, objectless sense of yearning, an emptiness, almost a pain of misunderstood desire. The girl experiencing this says she is sick and she may very well be because this kind of yearning can be so intense that it is actually manifested as a nausea, perhaps as an inability to swallow. She may throw herself on the bed and sob her heart out or get angry for no reason at all. She does not recognize that the basis of this is sexual desire which is not recognized as such. There is no object, no conscious satisfaction related to this conflict and frustration, so she handles it by explosion.

This could be the case with many young sisters entering the religious life. During the novitiate they are preoccupied with its daily demands and in the post-novitiate years with their studies, and during these years there is not a single day when they can turn in and look at themselves and hence they do not have to face this problem. This leaves them vulnerable. When the problem is handled in this way the young sister gets into another kind of latency period, the sexual problem subsiding for a while.

Then come the thirties. The full flowering of organic maturity runs from about twenty-two to thirty-two. And all the processes that are identified now as senescence begin in the early thirties. Besides this, the organism makes another violent attack. A most extraordinary thing about women is that they do not know about this. The peak time of sexual demand is in the period from thirty to thirty-five. The organism reaches a plateau of maturity and realizes, if the individual does not, that it is going down-hill. (A man is in a slightly different rhythm in this matter, but for the woman this is a peak period of maximal disturbance). Once again one can see the infantile patterns emerging—she gets disturbed, she has recourse to tantrums, quarrels, fights, negativism, etc. If young religious could only be prepared for this and taught what it is about they would be saved from making the gravest mistake in their life. This is to think that because of this they are unique or that they should not have chosen this vocation.

It takes a few years to handle this and it takes a great deal of choosing. Chastity is repeated choosing, but it requires something else. It should be possible to teach young adults how to "ride out the storm." They have been taught that the only way to handle sexual disturbances is to crush them out. You simply turn your mind away and say a prayer, etc. This is magic. There is no way whereby you can directly alter the organism. "Riding out the storm" means having a perfectly mature, healthy, cheerful attitude towards these things and being able to distinguish the storm you are riding from the voluntarily indulged-in type of sexuality which is a very different matter. The statistics show that the largest group seeking dispensation from vows is in the first half of the thirties.

13. THE PSYCHOLOGY OF CHASTITY

The psychology of chastity may be dealt with under three headings: what to expect from infancy onwards; the depths of the effects of sexual indulgence or abstinence on the personality; some of the ways in which we can change the sexual into interesting and attractive channels. The last two headings will be dealt with in the next section.

What to Expect

We know what to expect in infancy, the pubertal years, and adolescence. In infancy there is a great deal of self-gratification sought, the child wanting to be fondled and to receive an outpouring of affection. Just before puberty we can also expect the occurrence of physiological demands and excitement. In adolescence the mutual attraction of boys for girls and vice versa manifests itself.

It seems inconceivable that a healthy-bodied person could go through the major changes of adolescence without experiencing a good deal of curiosity, fantasy, imagery, and desire. There are those who are preserved from this by a special grace, but it is not necessarily a good thing to be preserved from these images associated with sexuality. In their twenties and thirties we expect persons to find themselves disturbed and troubled by this sort of thing. Some reassurance is necessary. It is really a difficult thing to commit serious sins of thought and desire in this matter of the sixth and ninth commandments, though we have been misled into thinking it is the easiest thing in the world. The spontaneous occurrences of images, desires, etc., is to be expected and is not even culpable if one has reason for dwelling on such things. The problem rises only when these are used to produce a sexual form of pleasure.

The second point is this: it is inconceivable that a normal person with normal endrocrinological processes and hormones would go through the growing-up process to adulthood without experiencing certain ordinary organic reflexes. In addition to a vague sort of curiosity, desire, thoughts, etc., the developing healthy body will at least occasionally experience various reflex processes. This is in no way culpable. Worth remembering is the fact that the vow of chastity is based precisely on the normalcy of the human personality. Vows of virginity and consecration cannot be made by specially processed alabaster figures. You are the living body. You will experience or will have experienced images, ideas, organic reflexes pertaining to sexual things. This does not mean that you are where you ought not to be, but that you are the type of person who could take such a vow.

Immature Personalities

The healthy developing personality will have a completely frank, clear-cut expectation of these things and will retain a certain capacity to comfort him/herself about these things instead of becoming anxious and disturbed. What about the anxious and disturbed personality, the person who is immature for his age, for example, the fifteen-year-old who acts like ten and the twenty-five-year-old who acts like fifteen? These are not unhealthy personalities but they are immature. They cause great anxiety to themselves and they will fall into one or other of the following categories: (1) the over-concerned; (2) the over-repelled; (3) the over-attracted.

The Over-Concerned

These make themselves unhappy because they are always worried about sin and felt-states of guilt. They are sometimes called "scrupulous." A number of confessors and spiritual directors do not know what scrupulosity is. They allow people to think themselves such when they are simply among the over-concerned. The number of genuinely scrupulous persons is about one in a thousand. Scruples is a supernatural trial, a temporary disorder of the spirit. It is a means through which a particular type of soul is lifted to a clearer vision of the spiritual goal. The same behavior characterizing the scrupulous will characterize the over-concerned. They get involved in wondering: Was that a sin? Should I do this?

What is the source of all this? It really goes back to childhood experiences. The infant cannot incur real guilt and neither can the child. Real guilt begins only when one is functioning as a rational creature, sometime after seven to nine, depending on the intelligence level. Though the infant or child can incur no guilt, he can feel guilty. He learns how to behave by being made to feel guilty; the mother withdrawing affection, for example, causes the child to feel guilty and to try to regain the mother's love. States of feeling guilty come long before any real guilt is incurred. The two concepts are radically different. The child may not be able to handle his guilt feelings. The mother, especially the overpunitive mother, can precipitate tremendous guilt feelings in the child which he may not be able to cope with. The child at twelve to eighteen months or two years has only two ways of handling these feelings when they are too painful. He cannot reason as an adult, therefore he will become rigid, meticulous, carefully avoiding action to see that he does not precipitate such guilt feelings anymore. He becomes over-conforming. The mother has made him feel guilty because he soiled his bed and so the child's little being is geared to not soiling it. Or he has been made to feel horribly guilty because he was exploring his body and the mother punished him severely. The genital area becomes "dirty," "horrible," "to be avoided."

The second means the child will use to avoid guilt feelings is the way of repression. The child can extrude the guilt totally from consciousness, repress it completely so that he will not feel guilty. This is the source of the sort of behavior we identify with scrupulosity later on, repressed guilt manifesting itself in different ways. The child who takes the rigid, conformity way out becomes a sort of perfectionist. He must reach the kind of arbitrary level of perfection that he sets for himself in order to avoid the experience of guilt-feelings. The repressed guilt can be held in check right up to adolescence and then it breaks through again.

In the adult years, the late teens and into the twenties and thirties, we can see these processes at work again, rigid conformity and repression. The over-concerned person at this age will set for himself an arbitrary level of perfection, measuring his attainment in respect to that degree of perfection in terms of rigid conformity which is in no sense either spirituality or morality. This is infantile thinking coming to the surface. He will say: "I know it wasn't wrong, but I still feel it might have been. I would like to confess it although it wasn't a sin." Why? If he says: "I want to confess it insofar as I was guilty," that is all right. But if he says: "I do not know whether I was guilty or not, I cannot work it out," and if he is over-concerned about this, then his thinking is infantile.

Another way this type of thinking comes to the surface is in the set of attitudes just mentioned, the use of words such as "horrible," "hideous," "dirty," with reference to things sexual. All these are childish adjectives. When we find ourselves shying away from the sexual or thinking in infantile terms about it, then we are not defending chastity. The defence of chastity must lie essentially in recognizing the attraction and beauty and joy and pleasure of human, sexual love.

The Over-Repelled

The second group, the over-repelled, is made up of those who have recourse to the mechanism of repression to handle sexuality. Many people use words like "repression" and "frustration" without realizing the meaning these terms have in psychological usage. Frustration is the unconscious blocking of the force of the sexual instinct, and repression is the infant's unconscious defence against the felt-states of guilt. To say that one is repressed means that one cannot bear the intensity of the guilt-feelings associated with sex and to defend oneself from this experience one crushes the whole thing from one's mind.

In our contemporary society we can distinguish different ways of handling the forces of the sexual instinct. The first and most obvious is "expression." This is evident in miniskirts, pop-magazines, pictures, dating, necking parties, sexual acts of all kinds. It takes many forms and not all are to be regarded as sinful. But it would be incorrect to say these various forms of expression are not sexual. Such innocuous things as sun-bathing in the summertime on beaches, men and women, boys and girls together, are expressions of the libido, but this is not sinful. Many forms of creative literature or art are expressions of the sexual, for example, the love poetry of John Donne, Shelley, statues of Venus de Milo. These are not sinful.

This manner of expressing the sexual is not our way as religious. We are bound not to express it in sinful ways, but we are also obligated not to express it even in non-sinful ways. In this connection the religious observances of modesty are not to be regarded as injunctions binding in conscience but they belong to this level. In other words, things legitimate in persons not bound by the vow of chastity will not be legitimate for those so bound. A mini-skirt is an expression of sexuality, and one would be surprised to see a novice in a mini-skirt.

Another way of handling the sexual in our contemporary world is by "suppression." It has had its day but it will revive again. Suppression is the way in which the Buddha and his disciples handled it. It was done by attempting to place oneself in the state of abolishing all desires which was neither human nor was it control. In the Buddhist type of contemplation, the *Nirvana*, their state of beatitude, consists in the absence of all felt-states. This differs from repression which is the damming up of the sexual instinct through fear of incurring guilt. Suppression is a very conscious and deliberate extrusion from consciousness of all emotion and this is effected by a voluntary effort. It is a denial of part of God's creation and is equivalent to saying that all feeling and desiring are bad. The good man is the one who can feel and desire but keeps these under control.

Another way of handling sexuality is "sublimation." Many religious have been misled by the incorrect use of this word. Sublimation, as repression, frustration, and expression, is related to sexuality. It is an unconscious process whereby the energies associated with sexual feelings, emotions, and desires are not recognized for what they are and because they are relegated to the unconscious these energies are drained off in all sorts of innocuous ways. For example, a spinster of forty-five, not recognizing her sexuality, or being terrified to do so, may find that she can cope with herself by breeding pekingese. This is sublimation. She is not doing this because it is worthwhile, but this is one way she does not have to face the problem of sexuality. Sublimation is a distortion too. An individual may be able to sublimate sexuality through a social dedication and services of all kinds. When this service is done as a result of sublimation the individual is often difficult, neurotic, and a rather unlovable person.

When an individual recognizes the attraction of sexuality for what it is, recognizing the reactions of the healthy organism, and that all feelings and desires are good, and at the same time says: "Yes, but there is something better and I will choose this. I will mobilize all my resources but will control them. It will be my free choice and I will choose that sort of loving," this is not sublimation. This is the conscious, rational mind evaluating and making adult choices. Religious are not sublimating in choosing the love of God and making this the motive of their work in teaching, etc. There may be some in the religious life who are there because of sublimation, however the religious life itself is not sublimation. The essence of being a religious is that one freely chooses to be one. One does not enter through fear of an alternative.

Human motivation is never purely spiritual or rational. We can expect to find layers of motivation, a certain amount of fear, attraction, defence, repression, sublimation. There is nothing wrong in this provided that at the top of the scale there is a clear-cut area of decision and free choice. What invalidates the choice could be seen in the case of a religious who literally knew nothing about the sexual or about its related emotions and who because of such repression could not face the world and sought refuge in a monastery or convent. It is rare to find this in such an extreme form. The normal thing is a combination of many levels of motivation interlocked and intermingled.

Coming back to what we were saying when speaking of the over-repelled, we stated that their way of handling sexuality was by repression. Unhappily, in the nineteenth century and to some extent into the twentieth, youngsters were taught the mechanism of repression as though it were control. The whole of the Victorian era is riddled with repression and disguised sexuality. It was this mechanism that led the Victorian era to teach its women that nice women did not enjoy sex, nice wives did not really like to live with their husbands, but did so because this was his right. Nice girls were always pure and modest but boys were horrible, seductive creatures. These are all myths based on mechanisms of denial and repression. Something like this may still be found in some seminaries and novitiates where, instead of being able to talk the matter out, the subject is taboo. The taboo mechanism in society is a social way of expressing the mechanism of repression. These social taboos have been largely eliminated and so we have a much healthier society in which it is possible to be a much healthier person. Sometimes "the baby is thrown out with the bath water." In other words, we may have taken off too many taboos but it is preferable to have them removed than to have too many there. There are some healthy ones and necessary ones and these will come back. God is perhaps allowing us a kind of bonus where we can deal with things with which our parents and grandparents could not deal. We can be much healthier in choosing virginity or celibacy than our ancestors were. They were aided by all sorts of processes and we have to make a much more clear-cut decision.

The Over-Attracted

The over-attracted are not usually found in religious life. These are the typical adolescents who find tremendous attraction in sexuality. This is not wrong but what is to be said of such persons when they find themselves in vows? In a very special sense such persons are protegées of the Holy Spirit as greater sacrifices are being demanded from them. We must remember: "You will not be tempted beyond your strength" (1 Cor 10:13). So the over-attracted in vows are persons with greater strengths to draw on. They may not realize this. In this matter let us remind ourselves that it is not the sheer strength of the sexual instinct that has to be taken into account. There are two sets of forces, the strength of the sexual instinct and the control it meets. An individual can have a very weak sexual drive which is met with a very weak control and this leads to problems. In another, a tremendous sexual drive can be met with great control, the person being in a magnificent state of equilibrium. We tended to think that the little alabaster statue going around without a spark of femininity in her was the better sort of sister. The reason for this was that she was easier to handle. The attractive, explosive, ebullient person who goes around maintaining strong control is in reality a more valuable and creative person.

Do we prepare our young people properly in terms of what to expect or do we try to safeguard them by using the defences of repression, suppression, etc.? Secondly, do we really understand the notion of sins of thought and the proper way of interpreting even sins of behavior? Thirdly, do we understand the different ways of handling sexuality, particularly do we recognize the possibility of denial or of substitute or indirect or unacknowledged gratifications as inadequate ways of handling sexuality?

14. PSYCHOSEXUAL PROBLEMS

It is important to realize the effects of sexual types of experience on the whole personality. The long-range effects are largely unpredictable. Long ago St. Thomas Aquinas pointed out that this is the only area in which a habit can be formed by one act, i.e., the area of consummated sexual experience. What this means in modern terminology is that this sort of experience leaves a person vulnerable, perhaps more vulnerable to the experience of desire and more explosive in terms of emotion. Against this background we must consider the acts and processes that sometimes occur.

Masturbation

The most common act is self-stimulation. Moral theologians and psychologists are in a rather ambiguous situation regarding this matter, the former not knowing enough psychology, the latter not sufficiently acquainted with moral theology. The result is a great deal of confusion. Acts of self-stimulation can and do occur in most people during the growing-up process. This is not to be regarded as sinful when it is spontaneous or accidental.

Secondly, very frequently self-stimulation is not grievously sinful simply because there is no real consent or real anticipation of the consequences. But we must not fall into the opposite extreme common in contemporary literature. It says in effect that this is not sinful because it is so widespread.

Hence one must distinguish between two different kinds of norms, the statistical and the ideal. The former is that this is so widespread a problem that it is taken for granted; the latter, however, refers to what ought to be the case. Some moralists have begun to think that the statistical norm is the norm of behavior and this is not true. This is applying the social norm to a moral problem and social norms are not moral norms.

Thirdly, a habit sometimes arises in the sexual area which has tremendous force and effect upon the personality and a habit can also reduce responsibility. We must again be honest about this and concede that an act may be habitual and may be wrong when carried out but responsibility is diminished because of the impact of habit, not necessarily, however, below the level of grave responsibility.

Fourthly, a compulsion can occur and compulsion is something totally out of control. It belongs to the area of illness. Compulsions can and do occur and persons with them need psychiatric help. People should not be disturbed about this.

Friendship

We are asked frequently about friendships and allied processes. It is quite clear that chastity must be considered as a way of loving. Affection will arise between persons who get to know and admire each other and this is a healthy thing. But affection exists at many levels of intensity. The real question is not: "ought religious to feel affectionate towards each other?" but, "how affectionate should they feel towards one another?" Often the notions of affection and

friendship are confused. Friendship is the mutual acceptance by two people, knowing each other's faults, without
evaluation, and accepting each other in complete tranquillity.
Chesterton has said that the test of friendship is the ability
to accept another without the need of much talking. This
mutual acceptance is friendship. It involves other factors
such as readiness to make sacrifices and serve each other, but
it is not exclusive. Any two persons who are friends can always absorb a third and fourth person or can do without
each other's presence for long periods of time. Friendship is
a very mature relationship. It is easier for men than for
women. In a strange sort of way men can carry on a relationship of friendship without affection, while women can express affection without friendship. They confuse the two.

The type of friendship involved in community life will
naturally be to some extent selective. You cannot be on
equal terms of friendship with everybody. We should not
be too worried about the fact that people cannot feel equally
friendly with all in general. The point to emphasize is that
one can behave in friendly ways with everybody. This is
maturity at its best. The test is not: can I behave in a friendly way towards someone who is my friend? This is easy. The
real test is: can I behave in a friendly way towards one who
is really not my friend? This is where mature control of
behavior comes in.

Affection raises other kinds of problems. Obviously one
will feel affection towards people with whom one has lived
for a long time. Persons of the same novitiate-year will be
more affectionate towards each other than towards com-
parative strangers of another generation. Or one may give
affection perhaps to a senior person, not just to one's own

age-level. But frequently this relationship of affection is not just the healthy feeling of a non-possessive, non-exclusive fondness. It is a more devoted, more exclusive, possessive, and demanding sort of affection which means that it is the re-enacting in adulthood of the "crush" relationships of adolescents. In adolescence, the "crush" relationship is not unusual, neither is it necessarily undesirable and certainly it is not immoral. It is the normal way in which adolescents become aware of their development, identifying with a seventeen-year-old who is already manifestly adult though still a teenager. There is no creature more attractive than a person of this age. The younger person identifies with the older. There is a little hero-worship here which is quite harmless, but a problem enters when the relationship becomes exclusive. The youngster becomes dependent on the feedback from the older one or else the latter becomes too possessive of the other's personality..

Affectionate relationships in the religious life are not unhealthy, undesirable or bad, but they may reach the stage of becoming a re-enactment of this "crush" relationship. This can be identified by clues, such as an exclusiveness which begins to develop, the appearance of an element of possessiveness, the beginning of a rejection of a third party, jealousy or envy because a third party is taking over, and finally, there will be seen a little "in-group" settling itself over against the larger group of the community. So far there is nothing immoral about this, however it is unhealthy and destructive of good relations which should exist within the community.

The relationship can now move another step. This does not *necessarily* take place, however it does in certain types of personalities. If the sexual maturation of one of the friends has already been warped then the relationship may belong to the homosexual category without either party realizing it. This can happen in a variety of ways, for example, the youngster may have failed to make the transition from the mutual acceptance of boy-girl at two to four years into the withdrawal phase at four to six back into the mutual acceptance of the seven to nine-year-old group. He or she may have been fixated in the withdrawal phase. In other words, either may have become the kind of person who can relate only to persons of the same sex. He or she is still not necessarily homosexual, but may become so later on. For example, in the pubertal years or after he or she may unwittingly enter a "crush" relationship at school as described already and in the course of this get sexually excited. What this means is that if the "crush" relationship passes from a kind of hero-worship relationship into a physical-love type relationship, the individual has now gone through two stages, the failure to get out of the withdrawal-into-the-company-of-persons-of-the-same-sex phase and into a second stage of being sexually excited in the context of another person of the same sex. At this point the person may now have his or her own sexual life orientated towards persons of their own sex. Such individuals are vulnerable. This may never cause a problem; it may never come to the surface, but they are still vulnerable and in the situation where affection moves into a love-relationship of exclusiveness then there may develop this homosexual relationship. This is where the question of how far should one demonstrate one's affection for another religious comes in. For the vast majority there is no problem. The problem arises where the relationship has moved through the phase outlined, affection becoming deeper and developing into a love-relationship, exclusive, mutual, and possessive.

This is extremely rare, but one can come across it in persons unaware of what is taking place. It is for this reason that irrespective of whether or not there is an affectionate relationship which has not got out of hand, and whether or not there has been a "crush" relationship in adolescence, there are certain guidelines that should be laid down. One of these is that there should be no physical contact other than that kind of behavior existing between brothers or sisters in a family. This becomes far more important when the relationship is private. One should not be puritanical about this. The real clue and test is: is there a desire for physical contact to the point that would give rise to sexual feelings?

Inadequate Ways of Handling Sexuality

Repression — Among the ways sexuality is handled there are some that should be noted once more. The first is repression. Many youngsters can grow up through adolescence and adulthood holding the sexual at bay not by control but by denial, by unconscious rejection, while at the same time being sexually excited or attracted by the experience of frightening desire, bewilderment. Sometimes the sexual will be then totally repressed and is apparently causing no problem. But it remains active. One of the ways it emerges is in the form of physical symptoms of one kind or another. This is called polymorphous sexuality. It can take any one of a million forms. You may find religious who get frightful headaches which "bind the back of the skull with iron bands," or who lose their voice and cannot talk, aphonia, the easiest of all symptoms to produce, relaxed throat. The doctor is called in and he handles this for them. Then they cannot swallow, become nauseated when they eat, so the physician comes in and examines the alimentary canal. Later, they have a pain in the stomach and it is doubtful whether they have an ulcer or something else and another specialist must be consulted. Free-floating symptoms of this kind are a warning signal that these persons are not terribly mature and have to learn how to handle their sexuality. It is not physical illness; it is a straightforward way of defensively handling one's masculinity or femininity. This is known as hysteria. It is a long-drawn-out sort of misery where the individual cannot identify what the suffering is and so attempts to localize it in symptoms of this kind.

Misreading of Biological Processes — Another way of handling sexuality—this applies to women—is the immature way of not understanding ordinary gynaecological processes. Some refuse to recognize that sexual fantasies and desires and feelings will normally be somehow related to the menstrual period in a healthy woman and very often in a predictable way. A few days beforehand a woman will get crotchety and difficult and maybe think there is something wrong with her. This is a biological, biochemical process and it is perfectly normal. The healthier one's attitude the better. Sometimes if it is not recognized for what it is it can be experienced as severe pain. This can reach the stage of being very troublesome. This is conversion again, not now into a physical symptom, of a pleasurable sensation into a self-punitive pain. Because the next move is this—sexual things and pain are closely related. Sometimes you find people who get a curious sexual thrill out of the infliction of pain. When this is obvious we know what it is, but sometimes it is not so obvious. We know it is a distortion if it occurs voluntarily. However there are subtle ways of doing this. One of them is to turn the menstrual periodic experience into a punitive process by not recognizing that it is a purely natural operation which can indeed be pleasurable. Some women get frightened by this and not being able to live with it, they turn it into pain.

Pain as Gratification — Another manifestation of this relationship of the sexual to pain occurs sometimes in the spiritual area. This refers to a small number. We know that sometimes processes which could be means of mortification can be used for a curious gratifying kind of process. This is the sort of thing that can happen where a person, not prepared to recognize a pleasurable sensation, can use such things as the "discipline" to enjoy the pain situation. This is a converted sexual process, a very distorted and unhealthy one, and it has to be watched. The "flagellantes" of the Middle Ages were banned outright because the Church recognized the possibility of distortion here. Sackcloth and ashes have gone long ago. In the Seville Holy Week procession you can see the re-enactment of pain. It could be a salutary experience; however, it might also be a curious kind of self-gratification.

Aggression — Another area to be aware of is that of sex and aggression—where a person is very explosive and angry. A very angry person, full of energy and drive, may not recognize that what is driving him or her may be the little devil of concupiscence. But one can handle it by getting very angry with someone else. Aggressive impulses are a way of handling one's sexual processes without recognizing what is taking place, draining off the sexual in this other sort of way. These processes can occur without the person concerned being aware that they are so linked. When a person wants to control this aggression and finds himself unable to do so, he must learn what the source of these feelings is. The only way to come to grips with them is to gain insight into the real reason for what one is doing. Insight is the clue all along the line.

Control — It is time to say a little about control. You can control only things which are in consciousness, not something orbiting on its own. The more insight we have (the more we acknowledge something in consciousness) the more likely we are to achieve control. Control is not synonymous with insight, but without the latter there can be little of the former. Youngsters in the city sometimes become promiscuous and impossible and cannot rectify their behavior because at a time when they had no insight into what they were doing (and therefore no control) the processes became habitual and now they cannot recover control. So insight is important. Knowledge is a virtue, the specific virtue of the intellect. That is why there is no knowledge to which we are not entitled, nothing which we cannot legitimately come to know. So the primary thing is insight. Next comes the recognition of the strength of the sexual area and the rarity of perpetual chastity. Then we begin to realize the task we are setting for ourselves. Think of the millions of people in the world and of all those who lived from the beginning and think how few of these maintained perpetual virginity, chastity. The rarity of chastity does not mean its impossibility, but only a recognition of the strength of the forces (St. Paul's law of the members) against which the mind is contending. Recognizing this strength is one way of engaging the enemy as you have to recognize an enemy's strength before you can go to battle.

Again, control does not mean denial; it means recognizing reality. But it also means relating our emotional experiences in all dimensions to their appropriate stimuli. We are entitled to experience emotion on three conditions: (1) that it is the emotion appropriate to a particular stimulus; (2) that we experience it in an appropriate degree; (3) that we have a right to it anyway.

If one desires to achieve control in the area of chastity, he or she cannot confine this control to the chastity area alone. It is only possible in the context of self-control, controlling the emotions. This means we must control our joy and our sadness. We must be sad only when it is appropriate to be sad, such as when one's mother dies, or at a funeral, but it is not appropriate to be sad at recreation time. Crawling away into a corner and weeping without cause is not a way of strengthening chastity. Control must relate to the emotion and its appropriate stimulus. One must be angry only when he can be "angry without sin," and this is difficult. There are things we can be angry about such as cruelty to children, the bombing of innocent people, the existence of sin in the world, but we are not entitled to be angry with others just because we do not like what they are doing.

Joy — We can be joyful too. "Rejoice with those who rejoice...," but in this passage from St. Paul we are told to do this in moderation, in a controlled way. If we begin to control our emotions in all their dimensions and relate them to their appropriate objects we are then bringing our life under control. But when the emotion is appropriate and the degree is appropriate there must still be a right to the emotion. To indulge in some emotional outburst to which we have no right can impede our spiritual progress and even lead to sin. And this applies in the sexual area too.

We must not have recourse to magical processes to enable us to deal with sexual problems. We are told that if only we said our prayers properly we would not be tempted. So we say our prayers but still find ourselves being tempted. Then we think we did not pray hard enough. This is bad theology. Saying your prayers properly is not going to remove temptation, but it will help you to handle temptation when it comes. Or we are told: Keep the rule and go to the sacraments and you will have peace of soul. But having done this many still have no peace and come to the conclusion that their virtuous activity is not being rewarded, that perhaps they should not be in the religious life. The *experienced* peace of tranquillity and freedom from problems is not the reward of prayer, the reception of the sacraments, or the practice of the rule, though a good deal of spiritual literature tells us that it is. Prayer, if taken seriously, the spiritual life itself, even if lived flawlessly, can and will generate anxiety. "The beginning of wisdom is the fear of the Lord." If we are looking for tranquillity and freedom from any sort of emotional problem we are looking for the wrong thing.

Abbot Marmion tells us that even when we are anxious or worried about these things there is the still center of the soul, rather like the eye of a cyclone, where one can be perfectly steady and stable with the cyclones whirling round him. This is the metaphor he uses for the *mature*, prayerful Christian.

15. OBEDIENCE

In the third paragraph of the *Decree on the Appropriate Renewal of the Religious Life* we are told that: "The manner of living and praying and working of religious should be suitably adapted to the psychological and social needs of our time and to the cultural differences." The importance of cultural factors is clearly indicated. If one places together the psychological, social, and cultural factors, one will understand why obedience now has to be thought out as an adult process.

We have confused obedience with submissiveness, passivity, conformity, and identification. We are going through an evolutionary process, part of which is conceding to young people more and more of their status as human beings. They are no longer to be held in restraint, passive and submissive. In fact these are not desirable traits. We have come to understand how the acquired virtues differ from innate personality traits. Virtue has to be acquired the hard way. For example, submissiveness and self-abandonment were confused with humility whereas humility is an exalted virtue that requires great maturity and it consists in knowing the truth about oneself. Similarly, with regard to obedience, some find it easy to be submissive because this is one of their personality traits but they are not necessarily obedient.

How are submissiveness and passivity related to obedience? There is no relationship. The same kind of behavior can result from totally different causes, for example, the child of eighteen months cannot tell a lie while the youth of eighteen years can have the virtue of truthfulness because he has acquired it the hard way. Submissiveness and passivity can result from what we have been calling "conforming behavior," but this is not the virtue of obedience. Some people can go through the day without violating a rule and yet not be obedient in the true sense. It is easier for passive and submissive persons to learn patterns of behavior than it is for those who are dynamic and active.

Conformity

How does obedience differ from conformity? A better way of asking the question is: How does conformity become obedience? Suppose we consider the matter in another context. There are many steps in growth, each pre-supposing the preceding one and leading up to the next. When you teach a child you first give him language skills. He will learn the answer to a catechism question or repeat an arithmetical formula but only later does the meaning dawn on him. The early stage of growth cannot be passed over as the later stage must be grafted on to it. Conformity is similar to this. It is not bad in itself; it is only when we mistake it for obedience that we must be critical of it. Conforming behavior is a way of learning obedience. We learn that behavior is subject to outside controls, demands being made on us to which we must conform. However it is a mistake to call this obedience. An individual may conform for years and never in fact obey. When the two are confused we should not be surprised when the conforming pattern lets us down in a crisis and there is no virtue of obedience to fall back on. When does conformity become obedience? There is no set age. Conformity becomes obedience at the point where the individual can truly say: "I am going to do what you say. I will initiate deliberately this corresponding behavior." This is obedience in the scriptural sense as seen in Christ's behavior. He was crucified because he chose to be obedient. Obedience always consists in a choice made by the person.

Obviously obedience differs from identification as this is based purely on affective states. On the other hand, we find a good deal of identification surviving in behavior which is called obedience. We are like Chinese boxes—one inside the other, down to the little one in the middle. We are the outside box but within us are all the phases through which we have passed and the infant is right there in the middle. The infant wants to be liked and wants to evoke the feeling of being wanted or belonging to the mother. Similarly, there will be many who will find a good deal of this identification process surviving in obedience. One ought to have gotten over identification at an early age. It is much later before one gets over the notion of conformity.

Constraint

How does obedience differ from behavior brought on by constraint? Here we must distinguish between physical constraint and moral censure. The former is in no sense obedience and we have only to think of prisoners in a high security wing of a penitentiary who are forced to go to their cells at a particular time. They go but are opposed to the source of this constraint. Sometimes one finds constraint where obedience is called for. For example, it was used in religious communities to bring about orderly behavior by locking doors. Moral censure is a different matter. When the Church imposes the regulation of Sunday attendance at Mass as a grave obligation, this is a statement to the effect that there are two choices: Go to Mass or do what you will. If you attend Mass, then you are worshipping God but it must be a free choice. In order that it be freely chosen there must be an alternative against which it can be seen. If you choose the alternative, you are guilty of a moral fault because you belong to a Church that has the right to evoke this response from you. There is no constraint.

What, then, are the defining factors for obedience? Obedience differs from what we have been talking about by reason of the motivation behind it. St. Peter expresses this motivation when he speaks of obedience "for the love of the Lord." This is the highest motivation, but the motive could be a more temporal, short-termed one and still be good. It differs, however, from identification or conformity to preserve public order, or obtain personal satisfaction. Secondly, obedience is characterized by the fact that I choose the source I am going to obey; I select the environment. It differs, then, from submission to factors over which I have no control. We cannot speak about obeying the law of gravity. When one chooses an environment and decides to live according to its requirements, this is obedience. We are choosing not simply the environment but in a true sense the persons, rules, traditions, etc., of that environment.

Free Choice

An adult act may be described as follows: It is an act resulting from my seeking what the environment demands of me and my response to this. This act does not spring from subjective choices, convictions, instincts, or affective states. These are all infantile and pre-rational. When I determine what is required, then I freely impose this on myself, choosing to carry it out. The religious has the privilege of having determined this environment more so than any other human being. The environment—the congregation with its rules and constitutions—may pre-exist the choice; however the religious has freely chosen it. It is better to consider obedience in this way than in the older way of "submission to the will of the superior." If obedience means simply absolute submission of my will to that of another, then it would be in a true sense immoral. This is what our young people are experiencing. They feel they are not entitled to abdicate their human status. This does not imply that the old terminology was all wrong. It was a language appropriate to a cultural milieu in which it was properly understood. Our youngsters today understand a great deal more about what it means to be a person, what voluntary activity is, and how it is elected and carried through. We must teach them that obedience is not abandonment of their will, but rather a way of becoming more and more a person by the proper exercise of their will, by choosing and accepting the consequences of their choices. This is the only procedure I know for allowing people to grow to maturity. The organism grows anyway; the personality can keep growing and there is no way in which it will except in the environment of open choice. That is where "self" becomes meaningful, "self" as the initiator of action and as the autonomous and responsible agent. The virtue of obedience lies in the correct discovery of the "self" as the initiator of acts.

What "self" are we speaking about? Not the self of the infant which is wholly self-centered; not the adolescent self which is unstructured. The self to be true to is the one I ought to be and this is where Christianity comes in. That is why the world cannot understand religious. For the world there is no such thing as the "self I ought to be," but the self I actually am. What counts is what I am. In a consideration of obedience this is ridiculous, for what really counts is what I ought to be. This is the projection of the ideal self in the Christian self.

Role of the Superior

Obedience lies in one's choosing an environment and consists in deciding the criteria which will determine what one is to do. Here you have the "self" at work deciding the criteria and this is where conscience comes in. Among the criteria the religious uses and the lay person does not use is precisely the question of authority-figures. The lay person in adulthood does not use authority-figures in the same way. He will have certain reference-groups to which he appeals for feedback in determining what he ought to do. For example, if he is a manager of an industrial plant, he will wonder what other managers do in these circumstances and determine his behavior accordingly. Always there is the reference for feedback. He can say: "I know what other managers would do, but I am not obliged to do that. I will go my way." He has an avenue open, an escape-hatch. Religious not only have certain determined authority-figures. They have built into their relationship with them a dimension which does not exist for the lay person. The religious, in effect, says in advance: "I am going to set you up, not just as a guideline but as a criterion to determine what I ought to do. I have that extra criterion built into my choices and obedience comes in when I apply it along with other criteria, for example, what does the environment demand? What is the role of the authority-figure in the environment? What other factors have I voluntarily opted into? And how many of these factors have I antecedently set up as determinants of my behavior? As you can see, among these are in fact authority-roles. I have decided to set up an authority-role as one of the determinants of what I ought to do." Many youngsters are at first confused about this. They tend to think in terms of the liberty of the free man and so they think that, although they have agreed to accept the authority-figure as a determinant of their behavior, somehow this is an abdication of their human role. This has to be explained very carefully to them. They differ from lay persons inasmuch as the reference-groups of authority-figures are not just set up as a guideline for feedback, but as actual determinants, as parts of the criteria for determining what they ought to do.

The next step is interesting: having set superiors up as determinants of what he or she ought to do, the religious is still free to reject. This means that one *can* disobey but it does not mean that one *has the right* to reject or disobey. This is the heart of the confusion at the moment regarding obedience. If I were not free to disobey, I could not in fact obey. But when you tell a young person that he is free to reject the authority-figure, he thinks you are saying he has a right to do so. It is a different language altogether. When I say that one is free to reject authority-figures, I am talking about one's status as a person; when I say that one does not have the right to do so, I am talking about the moral nature of authority. These are two distinct factors. However, right through the structure of the Church at this time you will find this confusion between freedom and right.

So let me repeat: I have set up the authority-figure as a

determinant of my behavior, as part of the criteria by which I determine what I ought to do. The very fact that the authority-figure is part of the determinants of what I ought to do implies that I might not do otherwise. "Ought" is always predicated on the fact that I can do something but might do something else. Otherwise there is constraint. Obedience consists in finding out what the "ought" says, and then imposing it on myself by choosing it, and it is in the choosing that obedience lies, not in conforming behavior. I can say: "I ought to be in by eight o'clock and I might as well avoid trouble by being in." This is not obedience. It is only obedience when I say: "I ought to be there at eight and I am going to choose to be there at eight." Obedience, if it is a virtue at all, must lie in the will. That is where the moral virtues reside. If it lies in the will, it can only be acquired by repeated acts. It is by exercising my will as an autonomous creature that I am building up the virtue of obedience.

We stated that obedience consists in a response to the legitimate demands of the environment. What are these demands? Here is a legal problem and there are criteria whereby legitimacy may be established. Should authority overstep the limits of its jurisdiction, then it is not a legitimate demand. If it is within its limits but I cannot respond because of illness, for example, obviously the demand is not legitimate. The question is: Who is to determine what is legitimate or not? Legitimacy demands that there be criteria and the primary criterion is the fact that the subject has selected the environment. If the demand comes from the environment, it is a *prima facie* case that it is legitimate.

Problem of Reasonableness

Secondly, there is a criterion of reasonableness. The unreasonable cannot be determined by any rule of thumb. We have to fall back on the virtue of prudence, for this is intrinsic to the virtue of obedience. In other words, you cannot operate obedience as an absolute or a legal concept. Unhappily, with the increase of legalistic thinking we began to hedge obedience round with a legal framework so that we found ourselves saying such things as: obedience is binding in this little area. That is why we must first accept the fact that authority is moral and, looking at it this way, we can say that all adult, free acts are moral and ought to be part of obedience. It is a grave mistake to separate obedience and say I am bound by obedience in this little area. That is where the vow comes in but not the virtue. In the precise role of being a religious, the virtue of obedience is the keystone virtue holding all the others together. For the religious the specifying virtue distinguishing the religious from the ordinary Christian is obedience. It is not something separated from the rest of one's activity. Taking the religious' activity as a spectrum, you can see that obedience illumines the whole spectrum of all the other virtues. They are brought under it and given their specific formality by reason of this virtue.

Obedience then differs from conformity or identification. The next step is this: by regarding all authority as moral, as both capable of and entitled to evoking and eliciting the response of the will, we understand that obedience lies in the will. Obedience lies in the fact that a moral authority has elicited the response of my choice. Obeying behavior, on the other hand, can be brought about by all sorts of other motivations.

The next way in which obedience differs from what we have been talking about is that I am obedient to the degree to which my choices are free from the infantile factors of emotion such as pleasure, reward-winning, punishment-avoiding, and subjectivity. It is only to the degree that I can emancipate my behavior from these that I can really talk about being obedient. This virtue must consist in my saying: Although I feel this or that, and although my inclinations are such and such, and though reward-punishment mechanisms lie ahead, nevertheless what I will do will be determined by the open choice of discovering what the environment requires and then, regardless of how I feel about it, I will do it. This is the mature man's way of running his world. The immature person decides what he is going to do by appealing to how he feels about it.

Why is there a problem of obedience? Where did we go wrong? Perhaps because we did not have the courage to rid ourselves of metaphors, analogies, and models, and think straight through to the sources. We used the analogies of conforming behavior such as school formation, military discipline, and even family life, forgetting that all these were based either on immaturity or conformity but not on maturity and obedience. The school model was misleading insofar as school is *per se* for the immature since students are not entitled to autonomous choices. School authority has the right to exercise constraint and exact conformity and these are only the preliminary stages of learning obedience. But we have confused this with obedience.

Secondly, the army model has misled us. St. Ignatius made obedience analogous to military discipline, but he was thinking in terms of his own life experience and culture. Moreover, he was talking about autonomous, self-determined beings. That is why the Jesuits are led in their training to self-determination, even though the model itself is misleading.

The family perhaps is the most misleading of all. Using the family and consequently the moral right of parents to exact conforming behavior is not the model of the lateral, horizontal relations of adults to each other in a moral situation. The right of the father to exact conformity is the right of an adult over the immature, the irrational, and the irresponsible. But the superior's rights in religion are not that sort of thing. They exist as the correlatives of the moral relationships among adults and there is no constraining power involved. We will have more to say about this in a later chapter.

16. CONSCIENCE AND FREEDOM

In any discussion of the vows one must consider the question of conscience and freedom as related to obedience and authority. The *Declaration on Religious Freedom* states that: "It is upon the human conscience that the obligations of religion fall and exert their binding force.... Every man has the duty and therefore the right that he may with prudence form for himself right and true judgments of conscience with the use of suitable means. In all his activity a man is bound to follow his conscience faithfully in order that he may come to God for whom he was created. He is not to be forced to act in a manner contrary to his conscience especially in matters religious."

This is a crucial point. It is the source of a great deal of anxiety for our intelligent young people. When we look at young people we should be careful not to see them through a screen that we project, considering them as the "beat generation," the "new breed," the difficult adolescent, the immature person, all the while judging their actions in terms of this image. We must learn to see them whole and evaluate objectively what they are doing and thinking. It is in this context that we want to consider the notion of conscience and its formation.

Freedom

There are some points to be made on freedom itself. Only the free act can be meritorious or virtuous, the human act has to be free to be truly human. There are different kinds of freedom and different limitations on freedom. Psychological freedom means that we as persons are ideally to be free from internal pressures from within our psyche or mind. And although the mentally ill person is not free, he may behave in ways we wish him to behave; he may go through acts of religion. The degree, however, to which he is ill is the degree to which he is not free. Then our freedom is curtailed in physical ways, for there are many ways we could not act even if we so willed because our freedom is not absolute. Not only that. There are many ways in which we could not physically act because we are not psychologically free to so act. For example, there are criminal acts we could perform physically but are not psychologically free to carry them out. It is no virtue on our part that we do not carry them out. We have been formed in such a way that whole areas of behavior are excluded from our range of conduct. There are those who are governed by prejudice in racial matters and this has been inculcated from infancy onwards. Hence they are not psychologically free.

Others are subject to socio-cultural determinants. If you take the incidence of juvenile crime in certain localities, placing a flag on the address of children before the courts, you will find that these cluster in predictable areas. These are determinants limiting freedom. The degree of our cultural deprivation is a measure of our lack of freedom. That is why the Church's mission is to teach people, elevating the cultural level. Here is the converse of that: the more we are formed in truth by education and culture, the higher rises our status as human beings and the higher this status the freer we are. Our freedom lies in the degree in which we have emancipated our personalities from the irrational, the inadequate, and the imperfect. Maturity, the achieving of full adulthood and mental health, our perfecting as persons, these are conditions of freedom. That is why our Lord could say, "The truth will make you free" (Jn 8:32).

Applying this to religious life, we see that we must enhance the status of religious as human beings, bringing them the freedom which is their due. Everything we do to raise them even in the natural order, in the socio-cultural dimension, in the intellectual life, emancipates them making them better persons. As a result their worship is improved. The more we eliminate what is infantile, irrational, primitive, and unhealthy from their environment, the more we are liberating them to behave as persons.

No one is totally free. Human freedom's limitations stem from the existence of other persons. Part of the dilemma in the religious life is that its members freely opt into limitations. They cannot have the freedom of the social isolate while choosing to live a social life. This has a critical importance because we are talking about a freedom that is limited. A point which later on will become crucial is that our free behavior is a controlled behavior in response to the legitimate demands of the environment and we human beings have the privilege of creating that environment. Other organisms cannot do that. We voluntarily chose the priesthood or the religious life and in so doing set up the environment with its demands. Hence we must hold two things in balance: first, the expansion of freedom by the greater maturation of the person, and secondly, the limiting of freedom by the interpersonal relationships we have opted into.

What about the free act? At one end of the scale we can point out the freest and most perfect act possible, that of Jesus Christ. His human nature being perfect, the Person carrying out a human act in that context was totally free. At the other end of the scale, the infant's act is not free. These are the two limits of the scale, but within these limits are infinite degrees. If we set aside the perfect freedom of Christ's activity, what other limits can we set up at the upper end of the scale? The answer might be this: a man who possesses all knowledge, is free from emotional and psychological trammels, is in control of all instincts, is not subject to social and cultural pressures or deprivations, and is free from temptation from without. What lower limit could we devise for our scale? We could define the lower limit as a person who is an adult but is now suffering from a psychosis as here there would be no freedom.

The Formation of Conscience

Now take conscience from infancy upwards and we can begin to see how it is formed. The infant has learned a good deal about behavior. It begins to learn to behave in response to the mother's training, her demands. At an early age he has extended central control over many areas of his behavior which once were not subject to his control. The simplest example is control over the excretory processes. There is no conscious control exercised, but there is control. Later on, the child learns another way of acting, this time consciously. He sees that if he screams loud enough his mother will come and give him food; if he is pleasant he will be rewarded with a smile. He is controlling now with a conscious element. It is still not a human act, it is not free. At about four to six years he begins a still further extension of control. He evaluates, judges his behavior. Such and such an act is good or bad. He is using and we teach him to use moral words to describe his acts. But he has not learned a moral category. He is thinking in terms of pre-moral categories such as reward and punishment. It is still not conscious so let us call it the pre-moral conscience. The child can say: "If I am a good boy will you take me to the zoo tomorrow?" And the mother will reply, "Yes"— and so he is good. Being a good boy to him means he will do what pleases you, and this is not moral thinking. This is what we have been calling conformity. It is an instrumental way of evaluating behavior.

This continues for a long time and we find it sometimes in adults. "I will keep the commandments because I will go to heaven when I die," sounds the same. We sometimes misrepresent our relations to God in that sort of instrumental way and then we wonder why we have failed if a youngster says: "I don't want to go to heaven, so why should I keep the commandments?" There is no easy answer to that. That is the pre-moral conscience presented in levels where the moral conscience ought to be operating.

The adolescent is in a kind of twilight zone. He is neither child nor adult but in between. He is capable of human acts but they are low on the scale. Remember the scale of the man with control over his instincts, lack of temptation from without, etc.? An adolescent occupies a place on that scale where he is not free from internal impulses, from emotional disturbances, he does not have the level of knowledge necessary for complete freedom, he has not had an opportunity to build up a set of virtues, and he certainly is not free from temptations without. Although he is capable of a human act, it is an impaired human act. An adolescent is capable of a fully responsible act, but in the ordinary course of human behavior the adolescent act is impaired by the absence of a formation which is his due. We ought to be able to give him that formation. We often-times have failed to give it and so it is we who are responsible for his delinquent acts. That is why more and more we are seeing the relationship between the person and society in moral terms.

The next phase, that of the young adult, is the one at which we can expect fully mature, responsible human acts. Not that these acts will be at the top of the scale, but they will be high up. The young adult ought to have reached the stage of control where he will have mastered his im-pulses and instincts. Maturity can be defined as the stage where the person has reached emotional, instinctual control, plus his autonomy as a person. When these coincide then we can speak about free, responsible acts as good or bad.

It is at this point where the Vatican document on Free-dom becomes operative. Freedom of conscience, worship, "the liberty of the children of God," all these are predi-cated on that stage of human development where the person can perform responsible human acts, and not on the earlier stages. We have one criticism to make regarding the for-mation of our young people prior to and after their entrance into the religious life. It is that we have a great deal of fear within us of the fully responsible adult, hence we tend to hold such a one back from this level of maturity. "Look at that child. How nice he/she is. Isn't it a pity that children have to grow up? Wouldn't it be better if they stayed as they are?" This sort of talk varies, however it indicates a frame of mind where we over-value the incomplete person and undervalue the complete one.

In the current tensions of authority/obedience, superior/subject, we must face up to this, deciding that our primary obligation is to turn subjects into the most mature human beings possible in the interests of the religious life. The world sees religious life through a projected image that is false but has some element of truth. It sees it as an immature state. Religious are often regarded as immature. The world must take care of them. And yet before entering religious life a man or woman could have been managing a textile factory, and many of them could have easily made their way had they not become religious. But because they are religious, they are looked upon as "poor innocent souls," incapable of running their own affairs. It is this projected image that we have over-valued. And so we hold persons back from the complete freedom which is their due, doing this with good motives such as over-protectiveness, over-anxiety, etc. This is a mistake.

To arrive at the stage the conciliar document has in view we must form the conscience. What is the mature conscience and how is it formed? What is this conscience upon which we must take a stand when a crisis arises? There is no such thing as innate knowledge of any kind. Let us forget once and for all "the law written in the hearts of man." St. Paul's phrase has been played to death. He was not speaking of an innate knowledge of right or wrong, but rather was using a Greek philosophical formulation to account for the fact that the moral law was binding on all,

Jew and Gentile, Greek and Barbarian. All were bound by the moral law in ways in which those under the law were bound, but the Jews were bound by revelation as well. However there is no innate knowledge, no still, small voice of conscience. This has been taught for so long that we have led people into this mistaken view which is difficult to eradicate. There is no such thing as telling a person to look inside himself and there he will see his sin. That is not an examination of conscience and conscience is not a "white garment" on which the stains of sin are visible. Neither is conscience the "recording angel" writing down all the evil deeds we do.

Since conscience is none of these things what then is it? We must start again with the infant. In the initial controls he acquires, the mother inculcates certain attitudes. These operate as primitive controls, the child being made to feel guilty when he does wrong. The mother does not realize she is doing this, but she picks up the child, is obviously annoyed, refuses to smile, and holds him in an unaffectionate way. The child senses all this, feeling that her behavior stems from something he has done. On another occasion he will eat his spinach and she will respond by smiling at him and now he knows he has done something worthwhile. This is the beginning of his learning how to evaluate behavior. It is strictly at the level of the felt-states of emotion. This is not conscience. However the child's first experience of guilt-feelings starts here. These feelings can be very intense so that he begins the conforming process in order to avoid them and this conforming process is identification with the mother. The child begins to respond to verbal instructions, conforming himself to these because he knows he will experience guilt-feelings if his mother finds he has not done so. These feelings can be very mild or very intense. Similarly, with the experience of reward, this pleasant experience can be mild or intense. The child is operating a category of evaluation which is semi-automatic; there is no conscious choosing of behavior. There is simply the warning signal—the mother says: "Sit there quietly until I come back." He begins to move around and this activates the warning signal of guilt-feelings and he becomes quiet again.

The ordinary, healthy child in a reasonably healthy relationship with his mother experiences no difficulties. But there are some children who are over-punished by mothers who set too high a store on perfect conformity. For instance, we have all met mothers who were upset over their children's behavior, e.g., wetting the bed, breaking objects, scratching at the mother's face in a fit of temper. These mothers increase the guilt-load because they are insecure and cannot tolerate the child's lack of conformity. Their world must be completely consistent, logically intact, no cracks, no mess, and all this because they are "perfectionists." They punish their child unduly to exact higher levels of conformity. These are the children who later manifest symptoms of what is often incorrectly called "scrupulosity."

Constituents of Conscience

The first constituent of conscience, its first underpinning, is the set of felt-states inculcated in infancy. When these are healthy they can be helpful. They are in fact the feelings that prevent you at this moment from carrying out a series of murders such as those unearthed at Yuba City, California. You do not have to reason with yourself: "Will I take a man and murder him and bury his body in a shallow grave?

No, I won't because it would be wrong." You are guided by this primitive process of felt-states that excludes all sorts of areas of behavior from your world. That is the primary underpinning upon which conscience will rest. But it is not conscience.

Let us take the second phase when the child actively chooses to do something by evaluating it in non-moral terms. Unhappily, the pressures of our culture are such that we have all yielded to them and are now applying non-moral criteria in the evaluation of human acts. This is the first major distortion of conscience. For instance, if you ask people what they think of divorce, some will say: "Well, I can't say it is always wrong because I've seen such happiness coming from remarriage." This is a non-moral criterion. Again, what about the pill? The morality of the pill is difficult enough, but you will not solve the problem by treating the pill as instrumental to other values and evaluating its use by its consequences. You do not solve the problem by saying the mother already has nine children, and if she had ten she could not take care of them properly, therefore she can use the pill. This is no solution to the moral problem. This is a means-and-end relationship. It is thinking in terms of consequences of the act exactly as the child does when he says: "I'll be a good boy and tomorrow I will be taken to the zoo." The consequence is the source of evaluation for the pre-moral conscience. This goes for many dimensions of our current behavior and thinking. But this is not conscience. It is the second underpinning of conscience. After all, this is a way of evaluating behavior even though it is not in moral terms. What are the moral terms then?

Moral terms are the qualities of behavior itself. That is the only meaning the term "moral" can have. Acts in themselves are good or bad, appropriate or inappropriate, as far as human beings are concerned and it is with that that con- science is concerned. Of course, conscience is aided by the primitive felt-states of the infant, the guilt-feelings. It is helped also by pre-moral evaluation. This is why massive research must go on all the time in areas such as the pill and allied problems. But the solution in the end cannot lie in the consequences, in an end-justifies-the-means doctrine.

You will find these categories surviving into adolescent and adult behavior. The statement: "I can't see that it is wrong to have premarital sexual relations if the parties love one another" shows the pre-moral conscience at work. This is the evaluation in consequences, not in the intrinsic nature of the act. Another statement: "I don't think it is wrong and I don't believe it was wrong because I didn't feel guilty about it." Here the infant's conscience is coming to the fore. The trouble is that some people have taught the young precisely these two categories of evaluation: "If you feel guilty about something, it is wrong; if you feel good, it is right." Or the second categorization: "If the act is conducive to a desirable end, it is good; if it is not conducive, it is bad." Neither of these is moral thinking and neither is conscience.

Arising out of these is a set of moral problems and con- fusions which are currently widespread. First, the problem of subjectivity which is enshrined in the statement: "Nothing is either good or bad, but thinking makes it so." Or in the sophisticated version: "If you did not intend evil, then what you did was not wrong; if you intended a good consequence, what you did was right." It is on the latter basis, for ex- ample, that people are trying to legitimize such things as "mercy killing."

The first thing we must stress for young people with

regard to obedience is that conscience does not mean subjectivity of judgment. This is very difficult to explain because, at first reading, what the *Declaration on Religious Freedom* seems to be saying about conscience, and what many seem to be saying, is that it lies precisely in the individual's subjective judgment. Subjectivity of judgment is subject to all kinds of limitations on freedom, while conscience is predicated on the freeing of the human being from the limitations we have been talking about. For example, prejudice inculcated during infancy may lead to subjectivity of judgment which we may then wrongly think of as conscience and act accordingly. This is the case with racial prejudice. In a classic research done in Tennessee some years ago, children were asked: "Were you told not to play with colored children?" and they answered: "Yes." When the parents were asked whether they forbade their children to play with these colored children, they answered that they did not. Both were telling the truth. The parents had not made the prohibition, however they had inculcated, at emotional levels, sets of prejudices received as prohibitions and which later operated to determine attitudes. That sort of attitude can and did lead to the murder of a Martin Luther King. One cannot say that such a mode of acting would be acting according to one's conscience. A person may say: "I had to do it because...," and he will give all sorts of reasons. He is not following his conscience but is subject to psychological pressures of a non-rational nature. These pressures are not conscience.

Secondly, conscience is not a felt-state of certitude or conviction. Many young people will say: "I know," and when you ask: "How do you know?" they will answer: "I just know. I feel certain. I feel it in my bones." When you hear this kind of repeated statement you know this is not conscience because, whatever else it is, conscience is a process supported by evidence. This is the second criterion for conscience. It is not felt-states, subjective judgment, depth of conviction, certitude.

Conscience begins to operate when the person commences to identify the quality of his acts. This begins in a rudimentary way at about six to eight. The child understands that regardless of reward or punishment, the satisfaction accruing to him, the guilt-feelings he has, what he has done is wrong. There is a rudimentary dawning of this in terms of the experience of hatred. The child is frightened by his own hatred, anger, aggressiveness. These are the beginnings of conscience in a rudimentary way much the same as the beginnings of mathematical thinking occur when the child begins to formulate the concept of number. It is not mathematical thinking if he is aware only of magnitude, understanding that the whole cake is larger than its piece. This is perceptual thinking. When he begins to see that if he has six pennies he cannot spend seven, this is rudimentary mathematical thinking analogous to rudimentary moral thinking. There is no innate knowledge of his role and there is no innate knowledge whereby he judges his acts. He has to learn to categorize them and this process goes on for a long time.

The conscience we should be guided by is not the rudimentary conscience of the child evaluating in elementary terms, nor the adolescent's conscience which is still imperfect and confused, nor any set of subjective judgments worked out from within on the basis of felt-states. The conscience we must follow is the one resulting from a prepared insight. This takes a long time. Insight is what one's understanding possesses at its best. When a man must follow his conscience this means he is to follow a line judged to be right by a prepared insight on the part of his intellect. To arrive at this point he must already have learned to identify nonrational factors and to eliminate them. He must be able to say: "I was prejudiced in this regard, therefore, I must discount that." "I would like to do so and so and I know I'm seeking reasons that will legitimize it." "I lack the knowledge necessary as evidence for my conclusion, so I must find the evidence." "I thought I had some evidence and find it is erroneous." All these are relevant to conscience.

Authority Roles

There are other factors involved. In determining conscience, authority-roles are important. Just as in the child's initial learning the mother's role is the first clue, and the infant's accepting and internalizing the mother's attitudes and values is a second clue, so, in the same way, will the child later on internalize its parents' attitudes and social values. He internalizes his relationship with other children, with his teacher, with other significant figures in his world. These are all ways in which the conscience is formed. The young adult, entering religious life, enters a world in which he or she is going to internalize still other clues to conscience. They will already have internalized something of Scripture as a source, something of the commandments, something of the life of the Spirit in prayer. Now they are entering a society where they must internalize a rule, a set of traditions, constitutions, and authority-figures through whom they have voluntarily sought guidelines for their behavior. They cannot have it both ways saying: "I have internalized authority-figures as guidelines to my conscience, but now my conscience tells me to repudiate them." This is the dilemma in which so many of the young find themselves today. "I am certain I am right, although the superior says I must do so and so." In this dilemma the over-riding factor is a voluntary opting into a relationship whereby he or she has cast the authority-figure in the role of a determining factor and it will require enormous evidence to bypass the authority figure as a determinant. There are cases where the superior cannot be bypassed at all as in the ordinary magisterium of the Church. You cannot bypass the pope's role and in conscience reject the guidelines laid down by the authority figure set up as an external control-mechanism by Christ himself.

Conscience is constrained by evidence and it is also determined by one's response to the legitimate demands of his environment. We have to keep two things in mind, first, the environment makes the demands, and secondly one's understanding of this determines the response. With regard to religious life the environment into which one has voluntarily opted includes the rule and all that pertains to the constitutions and traditions of the society including the authority figures one has decided to accept.

Conscience does not function until well on into adulthood. You will rarely find the adult of thirty-and-over appealing to conscience in the same way in which the late-adolescent does. The adult will have recognized the different dimensions of conscience and will have learned to discriminate between the felt-states of certitude to which the adolescent appeals. He will have learned to distinguish these from the discovery of his obligations by his intellect. Our responsibility is predicated on the degree of enlightenment of our conscience. The freer we are the more enlightened is our conscience and the greater is our responsibility. So we are increasing the load of responsibility by leading our young people to higher levels of functioning. This is where obedience comes in with reference to conscience. The more one exercises an enlightened conscience in choosing to obey, the more perfect is one's human stature. That is why obedience is a virtue for the mature and not the immature. Identification and conformity are the pre-moral correlates in the immature of the virtue of obedience in the mature.

Finally, our freedom is related to our responsibility. Freedom is meaningful only in relation to authority which is one thing many have forgotten. Many think freedom is to be free from authority whereas without authority there is no freedom. Freedom is the relationship between me and my behavior when the options are open. If there is no option open the act is not free. So obedience must mean a choosing where the options are open. It must be possible to disobey if I am going to obey and that is why authority and constraint are irreconcilable.

We have been tempted to identify conscience with freedom of choice. This is where young people have been misled. They are free to choose according to the measure of their formation. But one should note that one is free to choose evil. We choose evil freely and conscience can never bind in that way. Conscience binds only along one section of the fork of the road, so to speak, this way and not that way. But the young confuse conscience with freedom and choice. Conscience is the enlightened intellect determining the choice to be made along one fork. It is meaningful only in human terms and in the space-time continuum when the possibility of acting the other way is the measure of our human stature.

It is only because the options are open that we are capable of a human act. And conversely, the human act is a human act only where the options are open and that is the "liberty of the children of God."

17. AUTHORITY AND RELIGIOUS LIFE IN VATICAN II

We are concerned here with a world-wide problem, namely, the relationship between authority and obedience, superior and subject. We have witnessed in our lifetime a tremendous change from authoritarian regimes in the political and social sphere to a democratization of power even in eastern European countries. Let us state a principle which is perhaps the most radical proposition of all: in our post-Vatican II society there has exploded onto the scene a whole new concept of shared authority. We see it emerging in comparatively small matters such as student representation on university senates, something unthinkable ten years ago, and in such greater ones as Women's Lib. Today we are observing a change of the same order of magnitude as happened several times in the past: the change from the centralized administration of the Roman Empire to the emergence of local power in feudal form, and later in national form.

It is against this background that we must try to place the problem of the tensions within the Church and religious orders and congregations. There are tensions and conflicts, but these are part and parcel of being human. They are not tragedies. They exist largely because of social changes already mentioned and also because in the past we over-simplified many great problems. This goes for theology, philosophy, the sciences, as well as the relationship among persons in religious communities.

Role Definition

"Blind obedience," "abandonment of self," "surrender of one's will," and even the interpretation of the superior's wish as the will of God were common in the past. Such a simplified view of religious life made it easy for people to conform to its demands. Those who accepted such a view were people of their times where everybody had a place in a highly stratified society and where one learned one's role at an early age. This role-definition and relative stability were mirrored in the structure of the religious life just as other social structures were reflected in the administration of the Church generally. When political society was administered in a pyramidal structure with the king on top, the dukes next to the king, and then the local lords and squires and serfs, people knew what each one's place was, and conformity to that structure was the only way of looking at the world. In addition to the political revolution and the subsequent democratization of society, there has occurred another change of greater magnitude, the cultural revolution. The fact that literacy is taken for granted as a natural right today whereas only fifty years ago it was only fractionally achieved means that we are dealing with a more enlightened people whose horizons have widened, whose understanding has changed, and who are far more advanced over the people of even two generations ago than they were over the society two millennia prior to them.

All this is a matter of background to indicate that, historically, the Church has always reflected in her own internal structure the style of thought, the organization, and the attitudes of the socio-cultural milieu in which she has found herself. In her early life she reflected the structure of the

Roman Empire. The Empire's senators were the models for the title *Pontifex Maximus* given the pope and the title *Patres Purpurati* given to cardinals on account of the purple color of the robes they wore. The structure of prince-bishops in medieval times reflected feudal society directly.

Two Opposing Views

What we have seen in our own time is the Church reflecting two different kinds of society. This goes to the root of our problem. The Church reflects at one and the same time a relatively libertarian society and an arch conservative one. We have, then, a source of conflict. An example will clarify this. The *Doctrine on Religious Liberty and Freedom of Conscience* has its own history of tension between the late Fr. John Courtney Murray and Cardinal Ottaviani.

First, Courtney Murray belonged to a culture which was different in many respects from that of the *Patres Purpurati,* different from that of the great theologians of the past who had written about the Church and the nature of authority, obedience, and freedom.

Secondly, he had a better understanding of the hierarchical dimensions of the Church's life and this because he looked at it and at the European cultural tradition from a considerable distance and could see it perhaps in better perspective.

Thirdly, he had a different understanding of the notion of "development," especially of the "development of doctrine" which differed from that of Newman and his contemporaries.

It is important to note the cultural tradition to which John Courtney Murray belonged. It was a tradition which enshrined the attitudes to conscience, freedom, and religion

in one of the great amendments to the American Constitution, guaranteeing freedom of conscience to all citizens
in religious matters. That was in effect a guarantee made in
the secular sphere some two hundred years before the principle now embraced by Vatican II, the principle which has
rocked many structures in the Church and shaken the confidence of some superiors. By "development" Courtney Murray did not mean adding new concepts or principles of theology. Nor did he mean what Newman perhaps meant, namely, an unfolding of the latent content of existing doctrine
through better scholarship. Rather, he meant something
more like organic growth in all that was of merely human
origin in the Church's thinking. Courtney Murray was concerned with the temporal dimensions of the Church's life
and her position in time.

Let us take Cardinal Ottaviani's document entitled: *The
Duties of the Catholic State in Regard to Religion.* This
was written in 1953 before the Council was assembled and
it shows a point of view which we all thought at the time
was the only possible view the Church could take on a
number of problems related to our present theme. The
Cardinal was concerned with a question of freedom of
religion in a secular state. His argument was essentially that
the Church has rights which the State should recognize and
that in a State where the Church was in the majority other
religions were to be accepted only on a principle of toleration,
on the ground that error has no rights. This in fact was
enshrined in many theological treatises before the lecture
was given.

He tackled Courtney Murray expressly: "The contro-
versy recently carried on between two authors of opposite
views in a country beyond the Atlantic is widely known. One

of the disputants has defended the thesis we have just mentioned and holds (this is what Courtney Murray was holding) that the state properly speaking cannot accomplish an act of religion. An immediate illation from the order of ethical and theological truth to the order of constitutional law is a principle dialectically inadmissible." He goes on to attack the idea that the non-Catholic has a right in his own right as a person to his beliefs, and he says that we rather conceded his existence, so to speak, because we could not do anything else about it. He points out that the following objections are put to us (i.e., the Church's magisterium): "You maintain two different standards or norms of action according as it suits you. In a Catholic country you uphold the doctrine of the confessional state with the duty of exclusive protection for the Catholic religion. On the other hand, where you form a minority you claim the right of toleration or straightaway the equality of forms of worship. The result is a really embarrassing duplicity from which Catholics who take account of the actual development of civilization wish to be delivered." The Cardinal continues: "Quite frankly, two weights and two measures are to be employed, one for truth, the other for error." The case he is making is that we tolerate other religions as these have no rights as such. "Error has no rights" is the fundamental principle.

Courtney Murray's point of view is: Rights belong to persons. The Ottaviani viewpoint is: "The self-evident truth seems to be that the rights in question are to be found perfectly, as in their subjects, in those who are in possession of the truth and that the others cannot claim equal rights by reason of their error." The conciliar document has radically altered this teaching. It is not true that rights belong only to those in possession of the truth but to persons as persons. It is the concept of person that lies at the source of the authority/obedience relationship and this concept we have to clarify in order to understand exactly what authority and obedience are and how they are inter-related. There is no change in the essential nature of either authority or obedience. The change lies in the correction of erroneous ideas concerning them.

The Document on Religious Freedom

Let us compare the document just briefly glanced at (without perhaps having even done justice to Cardinal Ottaviani) with the document on Religious Freedom. The declaration of freedom of religion, the equality of rights deriving from the fact of being persons, and the evangelical source of the freedom of faith itself, these are the background factors against which we have to understand authority and obedience. Lest there be any doubt concerning the importance of this conciliar document, we should point out that Paul VI described it as one of the Council's major texts. John Courtney Murray points out that it is "a significant event in the Church's history." He writes: "It was the most controversial document of the whole Council, largely because it raised with sharp emphasis the issue that lay continually below the surface of all the conciliar debates—the issue of the development of doctrine." Hence the necessity of stressing the fact that this concept of "development of doctrine" is somewhat different from that of his predecessors. Noteworthy is the fact that this is the only document in which the following words occur: "... in taking up the matter of religious freedom, the Sacred Synod intends to develop the doctrine of recent popes on the inviolable rights of the human person and the constitutional order for society" (par. 1). It intends to develop the doctrine and it is the development of this doctrine of the rights of the human person and the right of freedom that leads to the current tension within religious life. This, in conjunction with the background factors already mentioned, namely, the change in the socio-political structure and the cultural revolution we have witnessed, is the major source of the changes occurring in religious life today.

The *Declaration on Religious Freedom* prefaces its teaching this way: "A sense of the dignity of the human person has been impressing itself more and more deeply on the consciousness of contemporary man." Subjects in the religious life have at times been regarded as less than persons. "The demand is increasingly made that men should act on their own judgments, enjoying and making use of responsible freedom, not driven by coercion but motivated by a sense of duty." This is what young religious seek today, that they be free to use their judgment and not be driven by force. They want to be motivated by a sense of duty. We should remind ourselves that in doing so they are in line with the conciliar teachings.

The document continues: "This demand of freedom in human society regards the quest for those values proper to the human spirit. It regards in the first place the free exercise of religion in society." In other words, one must choose the faith one believes in and the act of religion one carries out as a consequence. The document goes on to teach that God has revealed himself and the manner in which men were to serve him, but it states: "This Sacred Synod likewise professes its belief that it is upon the human conscience that these obligations fall and exert their binding force." There seems to be no doubt that the principle of freedom, religious freedom and freedom of conscience, is something new in the Church's teaching. We do not mean that it is new in theory, but that it is something somewhat new in practice. If we read Canon Law we shall come upon a whole section concerned with censures, punishments for violation of legal prescriptions, so that by reason of the coercive power (I am not saying the Church does not have this) conforming behavior was often misread as obedience.

The next point is: "No man is to be forced to act in a manner contrary to his personal beliefs and no man is to be forcibly restrained from acting in accordance with his beliefs." Both these statements deserve careful consideration.

The Principle of Conscience

The principle of conscience has been appealed to in a public manner by those who choose to go their own way and who are deciding to follow their conscience. We shall ask: "What do you mean by conscience and following one's conscience?" Secondly, what does the statement mean: "No man is to be forced to act in a manner contrary to his personal beliefs"? If these beliefs are arbitrary and subjective, has one man entirely the same right as another so that you have divergent and conflicting behavior between two, both of whom are obeying, each according to his rights? Is that what the document means? The answer is, "No." But what it does mean is a problem. The basis of this freedom, namely, "...that no man is to be forced to act in a manner contrary to his personal beliefs," is no mere principle of the social order which was Cardinal Ottaviani's view; a toleration in the interests of the well-being of society. Nor is it the lesser of two evils. The basis of the doctrine is precisely the inalienable dignity of man as a person. It does not mean merely freedom from coercion. The document is quite explicit, using the following words: "Man must enjoy immunity from external coercion as well as psychological freedom." What is meant by "psychological freedom"? "Hence every man has the duty and therefore the right to seek the truth in matters religious, in order that he may with prudence form for himself right and true judgments of conscience with the use of suitable means." This inquiry is to be free. "In all his activity a man is bound to follow his conscience faithfully in order that he may come to God for whom he is created." If a young religious reading this passage interprets it at face value, one can readily see how conflicts can arise. "In all his activity he is bound to follow his conscience." He is not to be forced to act in a manner contrary to his conscience, especially in matters religious.

Later on we read: "Where in view of special circumstances, special legal recognition is given in the constitutional order of society to one religious body, it is at the same time imperative that the rights of all citizens and of all religious bodies to religious freedom should be recognized and made effective in practice." The document is clearly concerned with religion in society and man in society in his freedom to choose his religious belief. But we cannot say that these principles do not apply within religion in the other sense, namely, the young religious is a person with the inalienable dignity of a person and he has these rights. He can follow his conscience faithfully in all his activity and must not be forced to act in a manner contrary to his conscience.

The last quotation is the following: "God calls men

to serve him in spirit and in truth, hence they are bound in conscience but they stand under no compulsion." This is the clue and the key to the doctrine on authority/obedience.

Let us now look at the notion of authority and power. These two concepts were perhaps confused in the past. Authority is always and essentially a moral relationship between persons. It is interesting to note that it is predicated on freedom. You cannot exert authority over inert matter, nor over living creatures other than man. Power is exercised over matter, animals, and unfortunately, over man. The two concepts do not necessarily coincide. For example, you may use a line of policemen to hold back a mob and this is the exercise of power. The mob is not recognizing any authority at the moment. But a policeman at a crossing can raise his hand and stop a line of cars and here he is exercising authority. Authority is the signal between persons which elicits a free response. Coercion or power elicits not a free response but one which is either such that it cannot be otherwise or which is brought about through the coercive power of punishment. In the past punishment was sometimes used in ways in which we would not use it today.

In all that follows we must study the different developmental levels and appropriate means of bringing about the required behavior at all levels. With regard to the infant and the child who have not attained the functional level of persons, authority is not the way to bring about conforming behavior. The child does not understand the moral relationship of authority, hence the mother must use the reward/punishment mechanism to bring about the desired type of behavior. Gradually the authority role begins to emerge so that we have to ask at what point can we really begin

to talk about obedience? We shall have to distinguish between conformity, identification, and obedience. These three
dimensions have often been confused. The same piece of
behavior can be produced by a human being for many different reasons. A piece of behavior which in one dimension
could be obedience might very well be mere conformity
in another dimension and in a third the result of straight
identification with the authority figure. We shall be concerned with the maturation process and how it is related
to obedience. We shall perhaps see that this process has
gone on at a pace faster than we in the upper-brackets of life
have been prepared to admit. So we still tend to exact
conforming behavior miscalling it obedience and the youngsters rebel because they really want to obey but not just
conform in an immature, childish way.

Obedience is a virtue for a very mature person, not for
the child, the adolescent, not even the young adult. Obedience is a function for the human person at a maximum
level of development. This is the change, I think, in our
understanding of what obedience is. It is not a change in
the moral nature of authority nor in the obligation to obey.

18. "SUBJECTS"

We have already considered the tensions in the Church at large between authority and obedience. These tensions we have based on a real change in the notion of the person's freedom relative to the type of worship God expects from his human creatures. There is a simple way of expressing this: God could have created us so that we would never do any wrong and would worship him at all times. The rest of creation does this, for its mere existence shows forth God's glory and this is what worship really means.

Free Intelligent Beings

The reason we differ from other creatures is that God willed that we worship him as free and intelligent beings. This is where the real problem of obedience lies for the "subject" in the religious life. Obedience must be free and it must be possible to disobey. This does not mean that the possibility of doing good is conditioned only on the possibility of doing evil. This is not true as God is free "par excellence" and yet can do no evil. The angels are hallowed in grace, can do no evil, and yet they too are free. Man is conditioned in space and time, and this condition is such that man can do wrong but is asked to do good; he can reject but is asked to accept. It is in this sense that we should consider obedience as the correlative of disobedience. In exactly the same way, we have to see faith as the correlative of the rejection of Christ. If there is no possibility of rejecting, neither is there the possibility of the choice of faith in the human condition. People who cannot reject Christ are infants, those with an I.Q. below 50 or 45, schizophrenics, etc. Because they cannot reject, neither can they make an explicit act of faith. These persons are singularly hallowed in grace, for they can do no wrong. But precisely because they can do no wrong neither can they carry out the free acts of doing right. Theirs is not the fully human condition. The human condition is summed up in Christ's question: "Will you also go away?" and Peter's answer: "Lord, to whom shall we go?" (Jn 6:67-68). This is the complete, open choice, without persuasion, coercion, compulsion.

Let us consider now the problem of authority and obedience from the subject's viewpoint. Here are a few preliminary and basic principles. First, freedom is meaningful in reference to authority. When something is free from all controls and rules it is equivalent to saying it cannot be free. The whole universe, other than man, is subject not to authority but power, such as the laws of gravity, physics, etc. Freedom and authority are correlative concepts. Freedom does not mean the absence of law or rule but a special kind of relationship to another person.

Secondly, and this principle is very ancient, one cannot make people good through legislation. Plato, the Greek philosopher, enunciated this principle over two thousand years ago. We still think, however, that if only we enforced enough laws people would be good. What the law brings about is not obedience but conformity.

Thirdly, teachers, parents and superiors have often manipulated the conscience of those under them in a somewhat pharisaical way. For example, the mother who tells her child to go to confession because the child has lied is manipulating the child's conscience to bring about conforming behavior. Again, have you ever as teachers allowed a child to feel that a breach of rule such as talking in class, spilling ink on the floor or coming late to school is disobedience? The child confesses disobedience when there is perhaps no moral fault. We have used the sin of disobedience as a useful control mechanism to bring about the kind of behavior we want from the child. We have also permitted children to think it is the "letter of the law" that counts. This we have done at all levels, and this is part of the reappraisal and self-analysis going on in the Church today. Find out what the Rule says and follow its minimal demands and you are safe; depart one "iota" from that and you are in trouble. This is pharisaical. The child reasons in that way and we should not go along with him. We cannot shed the child or adolescent we were, consequently our attitudes will be colored by such pharisaical thinking with which we have grown up. The more this is eliminated, the more our approach to obedience will be mature.

Role of Leadership

Noteworthy is the fact that Jesus Christ's mission in part was the emancipation of the Jews from the tyranny of pharisaism. "The freedom of the children of God" was what he wanted to give to the people. The first essential principle is this: there has to be a change in the style of leadership throughout the world. There was a time in a highly stratified society, the feudal society, when we accepted the idea that leaders were born, not made. The truth is that leaders are not born and moreover there is no such quality as leadership. Leadership is a role, a learned role, not an innate quality in the person. Some have the opportunity to learn the role of leadership, others never get this opportunity, and still others reject it. Being a subject is also a learned role and not an inborn endowment.

What has changed is the style of the exercise of this role. There is no possibility of a human society's surviving as such without differentiation of role within it. That is why the Church is hierarchical. It was not because Christ decided to found a Church with a hierarchical structure whereas he could have decided in favor of one without such a structure. Having decided to found the Church as a society, he then had to make this hierarchical. You cannot have a society without this differentiation in role. Unhappily, the differentiation of role was almost at once assimilated to the pyramid structure of feudal society. We had to wait until human society, "the children of this world," discovered the dignity, equality, and freedom of the individual before we began to assimilate it into our theological thinking. Then we begin to think we are advancing, whereas we are actually going back to what the Church was before it assimilated historical forms from a feudal society.

The fact that the style of leadership has undergone change is one of the sources of tension. When one has been accustomed to operating a feudal type of rule, highly stratified lines of communication down the pyramid, decision-making always reserved for the top of the pyramid, then inevitably one feels shaken when this type of structure crumbles under one's feet and one looks across the table at somebody who is now in a lateral relationship, not a vertical one. This is what the existence of the synod of bishops and the senate of priests means. Up to the Council of Trent, the idea of a synod of bishops would have been considered rank heresy because of the pyramid structure, and even Vatican I still thought monarchically in this pyramid structure. The pope is the single head of a single society. He really is. But the style of the exercise of his primacy has changed. We shall no longer find the "thundering" of a Gregory the Great, an Innocent, a Pius XI, or XII. Instead we shall find the operation of authority rather than of power by massive exchange on an interpersonal basis. That is why Pope Paul VI has been successful in many ways in bringing about a better understanding with other countries hitherto regarded as beyond the pale.

Part of this change in the style of leadership is the change in the theology of the superior's role. In the past the theology of the superior's role was that the superior represented the voice of God. Not only this, but two further dimensions were added to this role: a charismatic character and the "grace of state." There was the notion that there was an almost charismatic character in being a superior. While the style of the exercise of power in the traditions of a particular order was of human origin, it was seen by the subject as charismatic, almost analogous to the "anointing" of David by pre-selection on God's part. With reference to the "grace of state," while it existed, it was sometimes taken to mean a type of infallibility conferred by the role. This is not so. The "grace of state" has been the subject of many rationalizations and confusion in the superior-subject relationship.

The Notion of Disobedience

The final basic principle is this: we have consistently led young people to believe that disobedience is the only sin. Things are wrong because you have been told to do otherwise and yet you went ahead and did not do what you were told. This notion of disobedience, namely, lack of conformity to the Rule or the superior's desires and wishes has greatly colored our thinking about obedience, consequently our thinking about leadership-roles.

This notion of disobedience is related to the idea of the superior's representing God's voice. This is bad theology. There is a correct way of understanding this such as the subject's casting the superior in the role of interpreting to him/her behavioral forms whereby he/she hopes to live in God's grace. This is all right, but it is very different from the notion that the superior is by reason of office charismatically operating as the high priest did when wearing the Ephod and uttering prophecies simply because of his office for that year.

The above are the essential and fundamental principles to bear in mind if we are to appreciate the tension of authority and obedience from the subject's viewpoint.

Let us first distinguish the three generations in the religious life: A, those over fifty; B, those between thirty and fifty; C, those under thirty. Those in the A-generation sometimes have different feeling attitudes. Words have different emotional loads for them as compared with the same words used by the B- and C-generations. For instance, words and terminology in theology leave the older people completely happy, while these same words completely outrage the younger ones. Words like "hell" and "mortal sin" have been part of our language for a long time. We cannot understand how these terms can cause emotional reverberations in other people. The principle is that the emotional charge which determines the affective relationship varies from one generation to the other. This is particularly true of such terms as "superior" and "subject."

Secondly, talking now as a youngster looking at these words in terms of how he feels about them in the early seventies: suppose the Incarnation had taken place in an industrial democracy rather than in a pastoral, patriarchal society. There is no reason why this should not have happened as the actual occurrence of the Incarnation could have been at any point of time according to God's will. Suppose then it did take place in some contemporary Western democracy, we would certainly have different terminology regarding superiors and subjects. This type of terminology (superior/subject) is alien to the world-picture and view point of those under thirty. However, only two generations ago, this was absolutely normal because people were born into either an inferior or superior state of society. In a sense, subject and superior are an un-Christian terminology, but they have seeped so deeply into our consciousness that we sometimes cannot see that this terminology misrepresents the role. It is not inherent in the hierarchical structure of the Church that there should be a superior and subjects. What is inherent in this structure is that there should be a differentiation of role. What would the terminology be if we had to work it out? We might have some notion such as "administrator" and "collaborator" with the administration. In a big industry there are many different hierarchies, but if one started talking about superior and subject, he would have a strike on his hands. This is not because differentiation of role is rejected, but rather that the terminology, superior and subject, represents a style of exercise of the role alien to our contemporary culture. The young person entering religious life today is part of this culture and rightly so. It is useless to say we wish they were different. In the design of the Holy Spirit, this is what is happening and it is not a question of reluctantly or resignedly accepting an un-happy, undesirable inadequacy just because we cannot do otherwise. We must see these cultural changes as part of the "history of salvation" and perhaps see them even more clearly as a tremendous source of an apostolate.

The Exercise of Authority

The style of exercising authority in the religious life has to be changed in the direction of this egalitarian process. This in fact is what has happened. It is not just that a "new breed" has appeared, but the whole set of interpersonal relations has begun to undergo a swing through ninety degrees. Take, for example, a vertical line and at its mid-point swing it through ninety degrees. Nothing in the line has changed, only the angle of relationship. That is why there is no change in what authority truly is and what obedience is. The change is in the style of exercising the role of superior/subject.

Theologically, it is perfectly sound to concede that the exercise of authority in the Church will always reflect the society in which the Church functions. She cannot preserve the style of exercising authority from one culture in a radically different one. This can be seen if one meets bishops from different parts of the world and sees how they exercise their role in accordance with the culture in which they live. It is not a question of better or worse, good or bad, but only of difference. Since the Church is necessarily rooted in human affairs in the culture where she finds herself, the authority role will be exercised differently.

Speaking of the subject in terms of that overview, there are two things which must be stated. The human person goes through a set of well-defined phases of growth and each one has its own particular needs which must be met if growth is to be adequate and continue to full stature. The first and most essential need of the infant is the experience of basic trust. In other words, the child must experience the mother's trust in him. He must also be able to trust her, i.e., he must live in a predictable society. This basic truth is vital if the child is to grow. It sometimes seems that this basic trust is lacking among subjects. Instead of feeling this basic trust, what the subject experiences is something that borders on suspicion. For example, when a subject expresses the wish to do something and asks permission, even having obtained the "go ahead," the subject feels that simply because he/she asked the permission, in the superior's mind there is the notion: "We shall have to watch him/her." This is where the lack of trust or near suspicion comes in.

The next phase we are interested in regarding the matter of growth is the adolescent phase. The primary need of the adolescent is the solving of the identity problem. The adolescent has to learn answers to the questions: Who am I? How am I to experience myself? What quality has my "self" really got? This is crucial for the adolescent. We are ridden by the compulsion to form groups for the young. While they need group-structures, the very creation of these devices holds them back from the opportunity of experiencing themselves. The more they act as one of a group, the more they submerge themselves and become less autonomous. We are creating a chain of events which retards their growth in maturity. Thus the provision of these groups for youth is in itself insufficient. We do not even expect the abandonment of adolescent behavior until the mid-twenties. We are teaching the young person to hold off his autonomy, identity, and responsibility.

Independence and Autonomy

Subjects in the religious life feel that while the superior verbalizes a one-to-one relationship, he or she still thinks too much in terms of a group-process, a group-function, in which the subject loses his or her identity. To put it more positively: the subject feels that not enough is done to build up independence and autonomy. While these may be frightening words, they are precisely the dimensions in which God created us. We have so emphasized the notion of community that we have almost forgotten we are independent units, related to each other in two ways only: on the level of experience by external symbols such as words, and on the level of the supernatural, i.e., we are related in the "communion of saints" but this is not an experienced dimension. It is purely a matter of faith. In our status as persons, it is the person's prerogative to be autonomous, inviolable, and incommunicable. Some are surprised by the word "incommunicable," however the only communion of persons is in the

Trinity. There is only communication among persons by external symbols. We are totally isolated. We can think of our isolation as persons in terms of the soul in Newman's *Dream of Gerontius* at the moment of death. However, in spite of all this, the subject is not allowed to experience self as an independent, autonomous person, but rather as something less than human, diminished in stature by reason of absorption into the group-process.

One of the needs of the subject, then, in the current tension of authority and freedom, is some consistent feedback from those exercising authority-roles which establishes the subject as a person in his or her own right. This means being given the right to think, speak, express opinions, to be different and unique. Some religious congregations are doing this, but there are others where the subject who is unique is considered singular, odd, and therefore wrong. Being autonomous and responsible are somehow in opposition; having different opinions is being disloyal. These are unfortunate situations. One of the greatest inventions of parliamentary democracy was the creation of the concept of "Her Majesty's loyal opposition." It is only on the notion of loyal opposition that democracy can grow. And yet, any opposition within the smaller world of a religious congregation is too often automatically thought of as disloyal. We even use the word "disloyal" to express the idea: you don't think exactly as I do in all respects.

It ought to be clear that in all matters of temporal import, other than those established by the experimental sciences, the most we can achieve is opinion. This never reaches the stage of certitude, for if it does it ceases to be opinion and becomes prejudice. There are many areas where a legitimate difference of opinion is possible, where the subject could be encouraged to have a personal opinion which does not necessarily correspond to that of the superior.

Growth in Obedience

The growth of obedience is comparable to the relationship between a mother and her infant. When a mother wishes to exact the kind of behavior from her infant that she feels it should adopt, she cannot make the infant understand this through the words she uses. Nevertheless, she uses words and sings to the child and fondles him. Her purpose is to get the child to sleep and she accomplishes this. How is this magic effected? It is effected by the process called identification. The mother and child live in symbiotic relationship—two organisms in one coordinated life. The child identifies with the mother as does the mother with the child, and so the child behaves in terms of what the mother wants. When this takes place the mother is pleased and feels her child is obedient. In fact, the child is not being obedient as it is at a stage where there could not be any moral virtue involved. Later on, the child begins to discover that he is a little "self" set over against the mother, and by the age of three he plucks up enough courage to express this. When told to do something he refuses. This is the phase of negativism and there is no question of disobedience. The child refuses to conform because conformity is a loss of identity.

Both of these processes are evident in the religious life. When an aspirant goes to the novitiate it is like being born again. There is a regression to the infantile level and the Master or Mistress of Novices sometimes exacts a level of identification with him/herself. His or her attitudes, values, opinions, and standards, all that he/she wants done is to be done by identification with him/her. This is the "voice of God" notion, the charismatic role, the identification far beyond the limits of tolerable human personality. The young religious, like the child of three, goes through the same process of wondering what it would be like if he or she refused to conform in order to establish the fact that he or she is a person. One of the ways is by apparent disobedience, enhancing the experience of being alone, identifying self with self, being responsible even at the expense of disobedience.

The third phase is the adolescent stage when we get into a complex situation. On the one hand, the primary need of the adolescent is to achieve his/her own identity, and on the other hand, the primary pressures on him/her are to conform to group standards. So he is caught in a dilemma. This situation is much that of young religious subjects at the moment. Their real desire is to be recognized as responsible persons making free choices and offering God real worship; but then there is their status as subjects or as members of a group whereby a level of conformity is exacted from them which may seem to them to conflict with their real desire for independent action and free worship.

19. "SUPERIORS"

It was easy enough to take a worm's eye-view as a subject on being a subject. Now let us take a look at another view—we shall call it a dinosaur's view, looking down on all the little creatures from a height and talk about authority. We know what happened to the dinosaurs. They were marvelous in their own milieu, but when the environment changed their sheer weight and size was their destruction. When the ice-age receded and there was lots of water around and the ground became soggy, they just sank into the mud and gradually disappeared from the scene. That is why their bones are found in bogs and moors, and not because there was anything wrong with them!

There is no doubt that authority is necessary, indispensable, and sanctifying. It is necessary because we are dealing with first the great society of the Church and secondly the smaller organizations within the Church which need role-differentiation. It is indispensable because of human frailty. And finally, authority is sanctifying because of its relationship to obedience. While it is sanctifying we must always remember that the only thing which is truly sanctifying is God's grace. There is no automatic sanctification through authority or even obedience. In other words, there is no alternative for the grace of God. Even the best run superior-subject relationship is not in itself a guarantee of salvation.

We have thought of authority in the past rather exclusively in terms of the Church as a society set over-against other societies. In that context we generated within the Church a concept of legal structure and role-definition rather than role-differentiation. To my mind the greatest single discovery of the recent Council lies in the important document, *The Dogmatic Constitution on the Church*. This discovery is that the Church is more than a society. It is a way of being human and since the redemption it is the only legitimate way of being human.

Dimensions of Authority

When examining certain dimensions of authority, there are some things that come out clearly fairly rapidly. First, it has always seemed a bit odd that we geared all our resources to teaching people the role of being subjects. It is only in recent years that we have begun to train people to be superiors. This is true not only of the religious life, but also of bishops and popes. The long line of recent popes have all had a course of arduous training for their role, not expressly, but in conjunction with the other roles they were implementing preceding their election. In beginning to train persons for positions as superiors we have taken a leaf out of the book of management. When any great business concern really begins to plan for the future, one of the devices it always uses is training for management. Schools of management are instituted and have become the norm of present-day industry. By inquiring into the authority role we may get further insights into the tensions between obedience and authority, freedom and conscience in the Church at this time. As well as being necessary, indispensable, and sanctifying, there are also other aspects to authority.

First, authority is not an end in itself; it is merely a means to something else. If we consider our authority roles eschatologically, which is how all the dimensions of the Church's life must be considered, it will be seen that in this view authority roles will eventually disappear. They are time-conditioned, instrumental means, the purpose of which is the interest of the People of God.

Another dimension of authority is that it is sacred as well as sanctifying. It is sacred because all authority comes from God. But authority as the "voice of God" must be clearly understood. All authority is from above. We have our Lord's conversation with Pilate as part of the story of our understanding of this truth. But when we say all authority is from above, we are not saying that authority is conferred by God charismatically on the individual exercising it. What is meant is that God is the first and ultimate source of authority. And if we ask how and why, the answer is twofold. First, it is God as a personal God, and secondly it is God as Creator. All authority is personal, interpersonal, and therefore moral, and God as Genitor and Creator is the source. In the same way, we can say that God as "Being" is the ultimate source of our existence, but God works through secondary causes. We are secondary causes, not direct voices of God. The only case where authority is in fact charismatically conferred is on the pope himself. In the case of religious superiors (other than bishops who share in the jurisdiction of the Church) whether by election or appointment, it is always a transfer of authority between human persons.

It is in the role that we find the voice of God, not in

the person. The role of being in authority is an instrumental device to interpret the voice of God. The person holding this role does not possess any charism which guarantees infallibility. Nevertheless, the person holding the role has a very arduous task because he must render an account for those committed to his care.

Fundamental Principles

Authority becomes, therefore, part of God's way of ruling the world, but by human devising. As can be clearly seen there is an enormous amount of the purely human involved in it as well as some slight shadowy reflections of the divine. Old spiritual books are full of the concept of "blind obedience," "abandonment of the will," "abandonment of self." Quite an amount of this terminology which undoubtedly conveyed a truth has been largely left unanalyzed. We must remember that a great deal of it was metaphorical and was intended to describe a reality, but in its literal meaning it would not now stand up to analysis. If "blind obedience" were to be taken literally, it would mean an irrational and unreasonable process. It is in fact a contradiction in terms, because it would mean the non-rational, unquestioning, uncritical abdication of my role as a person, and my role as such is to be a self-determining, responding being. To obey, I must know what I am doing and do it voluntarily, otherwise it is not really obedience. The original intended meaning of the phrase was not the irrational thing, but rather the complete, voluntary submission of the autonomous creature, voluntarily choosing to abdicate his self-determination.

"Abandonment of self" is also a very misleading phrase. Suppose I abandon myself, who does the abandoning and what is left? This, too, is a contradiction in terms. What is involved here is not "abandonment of self," but abandonment of self-seeking, an entirely different matter. It is precisely the "self" that we love which has to be formed and which has to achieve the vision of God in the end. This "self" is "I" as the initiator of acts, and we must see obedience in the context of self-initiated acts, and not in the context of abandonment of self and pure passivity.

Just as in a literal sense obedience cannot be "blind," neither can authority be absolute. The only absolute authority is God the Creator. The idea of a kind of absolute authority is a cultural hangover from the days of absolute monarchs. Nowadays, absolute monarchs would not be acceptable to any enlightened, democratic society. Authority, then, is human in its immediate source, divine in its ultimate source; it is relative and not absolute, sacred and sanctifying and necessary, but still instrumental. There is a great deal more to be learned about it from the "children of this world."

First, we are subject to psychological pressures at all times merely by reason of the existence of other people. There is no such thing as "total freedom," something which the beatniks, hippies, or flower-people seek. The very existence of others is already in some sense a constraint on our freedom. Within an authoritarian structure, and all societies are this, one finds certain hazards arising which constitute considerable, psychological pressures. We have an example of the "power block," a group who wittingly or unwittingly rotate power among themselves as an "in-group." It is worth noting than any society of any magnitude generates an in-

and an out-group. The former is usually the power-holding structure, the latter is the "they" of the whole operation. When you find an "in-group" rotating power within itself, it is usually a bad sign in our newer understanding of the nature of authority. It is a sign we are not operating authority in a democratic way. The Church will never be a democracy, nor will a religious order be one in the sense of a political democracy: one man, one vote, majority rule. However, the exercise of authority in the Church must be seen to be a democratic exercising, taking into account the autonomy and equality of persons.

The following observation is another fundamental principle related to the question of authority. Things can be salvific without being ideal or perfect, salvific in the words of the preface: "right, just, and suitable for salvation," and therefore in no sense wrong, but still not quite what they ought to be. The implicit formal faith of an individual, who takes everything in the faith for granted, and never makes an explicit formal act of faith, can in fact be salvific. However, this is not what we ought to look for or to settle for. We should go further, just as Christ himself elicited from Peter an explicit act of faith (cf. Jn 6:67). While implicit, informal, inadequate faith can still be salvific, we ought to strive for something more perfect. The same holds for sorrow for sin. While attrition in conjunction with confession is sufficient for forgiveness, contrition or perfect sorrow is what should be striven for. With regard to prayer, while the prayer of petition is salvific, we ought to strive for the perfect prayer of worship.

In the same way, obedience and authority can be salvific while being very inadequate and imperfect. In respect to obedience in particular, the conformity is in itself salvific, but we ought to strive for obedience proper. In the same way, authority exercised in an authoritarian, non-democratic way can still be salvific, but it is not the ideal way of doing it. What we are concerned with, therefore, is not to reject ways which were in themselves perhaps inadquate, but to try to elicit a more perfect way of doing the same kind of thing. We know certain things happen to authority-roles with the passage of time. And perhaps if we deal with some of these we shall be able to point out how the exercise of authority could be improved by their elimination.

Stereotyping and Rigidity

There is considerable evidence that authority-roles have two effects on those exercising them, namely, stereotyping and rigidity. There are some roles which simply cannot be shed because of their nature such as the role of a father towards his child. In the same way, a priest once ordained can never cease to be a priest even though he may cease to function officially as such. Both cases of the parent and the priest are roles where the person is transformed into the role. In other cases, person and role remain distinct. For example, a judge exercising his role in court is expected to shed it when he returns home or when he is not acting as a judge. When he fails to do so, he becomes the typical, stereotyped cartoon character. Stereotyping means here that we adopt routine operations. It is very easy to set up a system and then operate it in an impersonal way. This has changed radically in our time, but there were many semi-naries where the rector and the staff were wholly unrelated to the seminarians. The same can be said of convents and monasteries. All authority-figures must be on their guard lest the role render the person rigid or inflexible.

On the question of authority, we now know a great deal more than was formerly realized about the result of conflict between role and person. An individual carrying out a role to which his personality is not suited will find himself in conflict with the role, sometimes with unhappy and disastrous consequences. For example, a woman who becomes a mother and suffers after her child's birth from a post-puerperal psychosis is one who cannot accept the role of motherhood. Again, this conflict can happen when the role demands too much from the one who has it, for instance, of a man placed in a high position in management but who lacks the intelligence and training for the post. In both cases, it would not be surprising if either of these individuals had a physical or mental breakdown. Role and person can be in conflict more frequently than we think.

The world is also aware of another dimension in the role problem. It is called "role shedding" and "role reversal." It is a good idea to shed one's role periodically, for instance, to go on vacation. This is one way of avoiding the rigidity and stereotyping we have spoken about. Role reversal is even more important. It means taking on the role of another while he takes yours. A very simple way to do this would be for the superior to say to the subject: "Suppose you were the superior and I the subject; what would you say about this problem?" The superior should then listen, and really listen, exerting no psychological pressures to bring about the desired behavior. A more important and meaningful type of reversal, however, is the abdication of authority and simply reverting to the ranks. It is far healthier to revert to being a subject and resume office later than to have a continuous sequence of authority-roles.

Authority Problems

There are some obvious facts about authority that must be stated. Let us put them in the form of a question: How does authority make mistakes? There are some obvious mistakes and some interesting ones that are not so obvious. First, there is the mistake of confusing authority with power. The state does this all the time and so does the hierarchical structure of an army. The power to achieve one's objectives or the power to coerce behavior is not the same as the exercise of authority at all. This has largely disappeared, but it is worth bearing in mind the possibility of such confusion because authority-figures can dispose of very great power.

Secondly, one can confuse authority with status. In all organized societies, the roles that society generates have attached to them a status-value and this in turn generates status symbols. Status symbols can be seen in terms of public life, for example, to be elected Mayor is to have some authority and to acquire a status. This status is recognized by the symbol of the chain of office, residence in the City Hall, etc. And these status symbols can become very important, in fact, sometimes more important than the reality and the responsibility of the role one is to exercise.

The third problem in authority is the confusion of authority with law or, to generalize, the confusion of authority with the institution. We know how the Council reacted against "legalism" and "triumphalism." The latter dimension is what is called status and status symbol. The Council consciously reacted against this and many bishops began the process of ridding themselves of status symbols. This was crystallized in the last act of the Council when the Pope gave each bishop a simple little ring to wear.

"Legalism" means substituting the impersonal automatic operation of the system for the interpersonal relations which are so much more difficult. There ought to be and there must necessarily be some element of system. There must be an institution, there must be a rule, there must be constitutions. The tragedy is that one allows them to jell. When the system jells then those in authority operate in an impersonal way and they are not exercising authority so much as power. When, for example, the law operates in a wholly impersonal way on the basis that the individual is not taken into account, it is operating the system as a power structure. There must be such a system; we cannot operate a complex society without a system, but there is no reason why we should allow our thinking to be affected by it. The confusion of authority, therefore, with the system is a problem. It is important to learn to abdicate the role of authority periodically, to exit the role, to enter into a wholly personal set of relationships and then to re-enter the authority role with no loss or gain, but as a perfectly normal operation. Other wise we are in danger of substituting the system for the reality.

There are other dangers to be mentioned. If we ask: What are the signs that things are not as good as they should be in a group? There are some good guidelines for detecting these signs. One simple device is this: suppose there is a group of superiors evaluating a situation. As they talk over the problem, note how often they talk about "we" and "they." This is indicative of the fact that something of the legal institution or impersonal administration has taken over. The *we* is the *in-group*, while the *they* is the *out-group*. This means we are not dealing with a society but with two societies related to each other and authority cannot operate in a society within a society. It must be a role within a society.

Secondly, one might wonder at the degree of difference of opinion that is permitted within our society. It is important to understand that in the world we have created we have taught young people that they have the right to express their opinions. For example, in secondary schools we teach the young to voice their opinions provided they can defend them. Within the society of a religious congregation or community we now introduce a cultural discontinuity and no longer expect or tolerate the expression of opinion in that way. What happens is that its expression goes underground. The result is that we place this diversity of opinion at a level where it cannot be observed and this can be the source of much tension, unhappiness, conflict, and unrest.

Another way in which authority finds itself suffering at this time is by its identifying itself too closely with the well-being, the successes and failures of the subject. In other words, if a subject goes wrong or if a whole community explodes, the authority-figure ought not to feel guilty. If we have taught our youngsters to identify too closely with us, then we identify too much with them and a failure on their part is termed a failure on our part. We suffer a lot of unnecessary distress. One of the most pleasing things in recent times is the way in which bishops can tolerate the defection of the clergy without getting unduly distressed, or even tolerate erroneous opinions expressed in public without slamming down upon them. This is indicative of a real revolution in the authority-roles within the Church. Authority-figures ought not to feel guilty with regard to their subjects' acts when the latter are exercising their freedom as persons, however erroneously. We must not become nervous about this.

The Exercise of Authority

There are some principles which may clarify the matter. First, all authority-roles are the long-range analogues of the primary authority-roles, namely, parenthood. So we shall expect to see something of the dimensions of fatherhood and motherhood in the roles we are concerned with now. Remember that the fatherhood of God is the source upon which all fatherhood on earth and in heaven is called. That is why all authority is of divine origin.

Secondly, in the exercise of natural motherhood or fatherhood one finds some clues to the difficulties of authority at this time in the Church. When a mother finds that her child has not identified with her, refusing to eat, sleep, etc., she becomes distressed and can even feel inadequate. Something of the same thing is likely to happen to authority-roles in the religious life. There are some superiors whose anxiety seems to mount to an intolerable level when a subject seems not to identify with them.

Thirdly, when the authority-role itself does not understand the nature of obedience, when it expects a level of routine, rigid, conforming behavior and does not find it, then it reacts by using constraint rather than leadership, power rather than authority. We had a good deal of this in the past. When one reads the history of Church Synods and the pages of Canon Law, one begins to wonder how all these laws came to be passed. Part of the answer is that when authority found it could not have the kind of behavior it wanted to bring about by persuasion, its nerve was shaken and it fell back on constraint. In that context, it might well be worth looking at some details of laws in constitutions, rules, etc., and find out where they originated.

An over-anxious authority will always feel guilty at the free acts of others. This is one of the problems in our understanding of ourselves. We confuse the free act with the conscientious act, freedom of conscience with freedom of choice. They are not the same thing. Again, an over-protective authority, and this is very common, will prevent subjects from doing good by the very mechanism it uses to prevent them from doing evil. Superiors exercising this type of authority will prevent people from doing evil by not allowing them to undertake anything on their own. In this way their subjects can do no good either, their behavior becoming reduced to some extent to the level of automatons. There was a time when people were heard telling one another: "Keep your mouth shut, sit tight and do nothing, and everything will turn out all right." That sort of advice is still given in military academies to young men on the political upgrade, but as far as religious life is concerned it is simply an immoral proposition. Yet many observe it. It is not true that by doing nothing you can do no wrong, and it is also misleading because it also means you cannot do anything right or good either.

Summary

You have probably wondered at times why the three vows of poverty, chastity and obedience were chosen as the foundation of the religious life. In terms of contemporary psychology we can put it quite simply: The person is the living organism. In the past we thought in Platonic terms and substituted these for Christianity, looking upon ourselves as souls dwelling in the prison-house of the flesh. We took the vow of chastity to consecrate the flesh. Now we understand more clearly that since we are the living flesh, the consecration of the person is also the consecration of the flesh. This person, who is the living flesh, is completed by possession, by property. We need things to reach our natural fulfillment. Hence we must consecrate the living flesh and the things necessary for it if we are to make a total consecration, and this is the purpose of poverty. The person is wholly incomplete without action since our reality lies in what we do. In the existentialist terminology we create ourselves by what we do. We can see the meaning of this in moral terms when we say: It is what we do that makes us the persons we are. In this most literal sense we have formed our character and personality by the choices we made throughout our lives. So for the finality of consecration we must consecrate our acts, the choices we make, the things we do. That is why there is a vow of obedience. The three vows are our inadequate way of thinking about one thing only, i.e., personal consecration. It has to be done in three stages.

Consecration in chastity does not make me chaste and consecration in poverty does not make me poor. Equally, consecration in obedience does not make me obedient. I must work at all three. In the same way, the consecration itself which makes me a religious does not necessarily give me a vocation. I have to work at the whole operation so that the acquisition of the virtues is the result of repeated choosing and it may take years of formation before this takes place. One could say that the virtue of obedience may begin to be acquired in the novitiate, becomes clear through profession, but may not be acquired until well on into middle age.

20. THE DISTURBED RELIGIOUS

In spite of all our efforts to form mature, responsible, healthy, happy religious, there will always be some who will require special help in the area of professional counselling. I'm talking here, of course, about the emotionally disturbed religious. Counselling is an art not a science. It cannot be reduced to a series of formulae, propositions, methods. There are certain pre-requisites, scientific insights we must acquire before trying to carry out the art, just as in architecture or engineering. This is even more important in the sphere of the religious vocation than elsewhere. Counselling is not the same as spiritual direction, common sense, or psychotherapy. It is a process in which a person is helped (1) to understand himself; (2) to make appropriate adjustments and decisions in the light of this understanding; (3) to accept responsibility for this choice; (4) to follow a course of action in harmony with his choice.

This is close to common sense, spiritual direction, and psychotherapy, however it differs in certain specifiable ways. The spiritual director takes responsibility, giving injunctions, setting goals. He judges and evaluates. Values, goals, practices, and rules are taught and their acceptance and observance are required.

Common sense is already aware of the answers, usually in utilitarian terms, usually by the application of some rule of thumb or insight acquired through experience. It is not to be decried, but it is not sufficient especially in the context of the disturbed religious.

Psychotherapy is concerned with curing an illness, usually by probing the deep unconscious and it is the privilege of the trained psychiatrist or psychologist to do this. It should be stressed that there is no connection between mental illness and moral fault, neglect of rule, etc., and that prayer in itself is no cure for mental illness.

The Art of Counselling

The first principle in the art of counselling is: Do not allow the person, his uniqueness, or identity to slip through your grasp. It is important that the encounter be private but not secret. Security is the keynote. The counsellor must be capable of great self-control so that no matter what is said should be regarded as quite ordinary. He should not by word or action register the slightest discomposure, surprise, or censure, nor should he show approval. In this, counselling differs from other forms of guidance, direction, or confession. The counsellor is not a judge and he should never dominate his client; neither should he allow himself to be cast in the role of a magician. There is no magical solution to the problems with which he will deal. Objectivity in all its aspects must be the controlling norm. He must never become emotionally involved, even through sympathy, with the disturbed person. He must cultivate empathy which is the ability to sense and feel what his client feels, to appreciate the true quality of his client's emotional state. This is difficult. One should try to discover whether the affective tone is fear, anxiety, anger, hatred, jealousy, resentment, regret, sadness, depression, or whatever else it may be. The first task is to wonder what is the real cause of the problem. It may not be the apparent cause. The task is to release the means for making personal and responsible choices and the ways of implementing them. Most often the problem with the client is not, "What should I do," but rather, "I know what I should do, but how do I do it?"

In the counselling situation, the client finds himself for the first time in a situation wherein he can really be himself. His confrontation is not primarily with the counsellor, but with himself and Christ. This is frequently both a discovery. and a relief. He has been living behind a mask, playing a part, acting a role, not necessarily in a bad sense. He has been endeavoring to fill the role of a religious, a novice, a postulant. His relationships have been in terms of his role and the role of the persons with whom he is dealing. Confronted now with a counsellor, he finds he cannot identify the role of the person with whom he is dealing because of the apparent passivity. This is what we sometimes call non-directive therapy, non-directive counselling, or client-centered counselling.

How does one go about this? One should begin with a few generalities—name, age, family background. Invariably, the client will say something like this: "I don't know where to begin. You ask me the questions." It would be fatal to take up this challenge. The proper answer is: "All right. I will. First, tell me how the problem appears to you." This gives the client back the initiative which he must take up. Do not be afraid of silences. Do not feel compelled to fill them in with words. And do not present a facile, stereotyped solution such as: "Pull yourself together, say your prayers, pray for guidance." These things are good but will probably not give much help. They will not help the disturbed religious to solve the problem if it is a problem of his role as a religious.

The problem, when it appears, is never unique though it has unique dimensions. If one is to appreciate its nature, one has to convey to the client that there is unlimited time in which to hear the problem out. This may not be possible the first time but one can always arrange for a future session. Always announce a definite end to the interview and never allow it to run into trivialities, for a clearcut finality and subsequent appointment sends the client off with a sense of achievement.

Most people have a need to unburden themselves from time to time, relieving inner pressures and expressing in words inner states they are often unable to face even within the privacy of their own consciousness. Watch for signs of physical tension, e.g., perspiring, hand movements, etc., and watch also for the too relaxed person, blasé, cool, detached, whose lack of affective tone may be even more dangerous than that of the excited individual.

The next step is trying to discover the problem. This means listening with the third ear to discriminate the real from the apparent problem. Sister has been taking librium in order to sleep, what is her real problem? It turns out that she is worried about her parents. They are ageing and she feels she has an obligation to look after them. She thinks she has a vocation, but she has been feeling unwell. What should she do?

This is the first kind of crisis we shall be concerned with, namely, the crisis of vocation itself. Such a person may not be ill or neurotic, though the doctor will treat her stomach and the psychiatrist her nerves. She has come to think that her moral duty lies at home looking after her parents. But the truth may be that she lacks the courage to affirm her vocation. This is different from assenting to it as affirming it is the function of the whole person, it is total commitment. She is holding back the finality and the totality of the commitment. She should not be persuaded to do this, but rather should be asked the advice she would give another in this position. She should be led to formulate the solution so that, if in fact she rejects her vocation, she does so positively, affirmatively, without excuse or rationalizing. If she makes the wrong choice and leaves, at least she has made it as a responsible agent and has not deceived herself into making it on health or alleged moral grounds. These are the dimensions that counselling seeks to highlight.

The problem in counselling is never unique. In general, we can classify these problems under three headings: (1) psychiatric problems; (2) personality problems; (3) spiritual problems.

Psychiatric Problems

A young man is striving hard to be a good religious, however he is full of fears, fantasies, depression. Some knowledge of the gross symptoms of the psychoses and neuroses can be of help here. Real psychiatric problems are not the province of the counsellor. There are many cases where the symptoms may simulate a psychiatric problem, but do not necessarily involve one. There are normal anxieties, conflicts, and depressions. There is even an area of unpleasant and painful emotional states, though these are still not morbid states. These are the corrective, emotional experiences of normal maturation, plus the productive disintegrations of the personality which perhaps used to be referred to as a "second conversion" and correctly so. One should not too readily concede a psychiatric problem. The whole person must be studied, not an isolated symptom, and particularly the person's ability to handle, tolerate, and live with the emotional state. The symptoms he is producing may be an "organic language"— the language of the organism itself making its protest in the only way possible, analogous in many ways to the child's organic language. The clue here is discovered by casual inquiries about the ways his emotional states affect other areas of his behavior, internal and overt, and by a close analysis of his real as distinct from his expressed attitudes to his vocation. Reassurance and a great deal of "supportive therapy" will often help him ride out the storm without much damage.

In general, there are two kinds of psychiatric disturbances, neuroses and psychoses. These are two kinds of illnesses and the difference is somewhat as follows. In psychoses the patient loses insight into himself and his problem. Sometimes he may not even know he is ill. In traditional terms "reason" is impaired or suspended. In neuroses, on the other hand, he may know he is ill but often will not know the nature of his illness. In traditional terms again, "reason" is not impaired or suspended but is under severe pressure. The vast majority, more than 90% of those suffering from mental illness, are victims of neuroses. Only a small percentage is psychotic. The neuroses frequently met with in religious are the "hysteria" and "obsessional" neuroses which can often simulate virtue or the life of prayer. It is important to learn to recognize them. Next come depression and anxiety states.

In hysteria one finds either a number of purely psychological symptoms or a set of physiological symptoms without any known physical cause. This does not mean that we should undertake to make a diagnosis. If you observe, however, a set of such symptoms in a client such as a high temperature without a physical cause, a sore throat without infection, loss of voice, headache, backache, muscular symptoms, or perhaps the well known: "I feel as though there is a steel band binding the back of my head," you should be alive to the possibility of neurosis. In these cases, the symptoms are real and the person is not malingering. The illness is psychogenic.

Compulsive symptoms are revealed very frequently in scrupulosity or in meticulous care in carrying out rather silly routines. For example, the person may be wholly unable to study or start writing a letter unless he or she has a pencil in a particular spot, a pen in another, the ink three inches away. Sometimes such symptoms may be observed in prayer or in the sacramental life. A religious who feels compelled to go to confession every morning or several times a day is probably ill and not on the road to sanctity. It is important to distinguish between scrupulosity as a spiritual trial and scrupulosity which is a form of neurosis.

Scrupulosity as a spiritual trial will appear in a reasonably mature and otherwise balanced personality. It causes real suffering but is based on a genuine will for perfection. These are the key-concepts in scrupulosity proper. As far as the confessor or director is concerned, he will be able to identify it as a genuine spiritual trial by the twin aspects that the genuinely scrupulous person will accept his ruling as an "objective" conscience and will be capable of obeying his injunctions. The neurotic sufferer, however, whose behavior may resemble that of the scrupulous person, will not be a mature, balanced person and will not be genuinely seeking perfection, but seeking some kind of gratification through his/her symptoms. He or she will not be capable of carrying out the confessor's injunctions. This is a crucial difference. The genuinely scrupulous person is mentally healthy and can carry out quite well the injunctions given, but the obsessional, compulsive person, by reason of illness, will be incapable of implementing the director's advice. Such people are not guilty of disobedience, perhaps not even of imperfection. To the degree to which any psychological illness is present, to that extent the individual is incapable of a human act. So it would be a mistake to hold responsible for a breach of rule one who because of the nature of his/her illness is not capable of responsible behavior. This is the "special grace" of the mentally ill. They are more vulnerable but not more responsible. We are more responsible because we do not have these problems to cope with.

The most prevalent illness of all is schizophrenia. It has the highest incidence precisely in the age-group we are most concerned with—seventeen to thirty. It is a very serious illness. The classic symptoms are: loss of identity (depersonalization), loss of a sense of reality (living in a fantasy world), and auditory hallucinations. "Hearing voices" is a serious symptom of this illness. The individual hears "voices" more vividly than he or she will hear your voice. These symptoms are real in the same way in which physical symptoms are real.

Sometimes it is difficult to know whether a state of depression should be classed with psychoses or neuroses. Depression in this psychiatric sense is the experience of an intolerably painful sadness, usually accompanied by tremendous guilt feelings. In the case of an individual living in the world, the sadness and guilt-feelings will be there, but they will be attached to whatever has seemed to be the most important element in the individual's life up to that time. A married man, for example, in a depression may experience this sadness with regard to his wife, and the guilt-feelings with regard to his children. A bank manager may experience sadness because he thinks the board of directors is going to fire him for neglect of duty.

When a sister falls into a state of depression she may attach sadness and guilt-feelings to the spiritual life, thinking God has abandoned her because she is a miserable sinner. If she has some knowledge of mystical experiences through reading St. John of the Cross she may think she is in the "dark night of the soul." Her condition has nothing to do with this, though the subjective experience may be very similar to the description of the "night" given in spiritual books. Psychologically similar subjective experiences can have either human, divine, or diabolical sources. Such depression is a purely human illness.

Psychiatrists distinguish two types of depression: (1) the first is precipitated by something in the person's experience, for example, the loss of a parent. This is called "reactive depression." (2) The second has no discernible cause in the environment but seems to rise from the soul's depths; this is called "endogenous depression."

Most people get depressed from time to time. In a case of ordinary depression massive reassurance can help. We should not too readily assume the presence of a major problem. The "endogenous depression" has no cause in the environment, it is not precipitated by some episode in our life. It is most likely related to some biochemical factors in the organism. It is essentially cyclic or recurrent. Sympathy, understanding, reassurance, maternal care, all are unavailing, as none will allay the patient's suffering.

This type of depression can be controlled only by a psychiatrist. It may mean the patient will have to face a lifetime of periodic depression, but we must recognize that it is a natural illness and has nothing to do with sin or guilt or any spiritual trial. The real danger of this depression is suicide. Never dismiss the threat of suicide as of no account, otherwise you may have a tragedy on your hands. You will not be able to annul the depression by moral arguments or spiritual advice. The vast majority of suicides are carried out by persons in an "endogenous depression" and they are not responsible for their acts.

One should not too readily concede a psychiatric problem. The possibility of simulating psychiatric difficulties is very great. One must study the whole person and not an isolated symptom and one must study the individual's ability to tolerate and handle the difficulties of an emotional state from within.

The symptoms may be within the range of normality. Let us make a threefold distinction: (1) All are capable of experiencing emotional states. These can be painful and many of the most painful states are within the range of normal human experience. (2) There is a range of neurosis where the individual retains insight and can understand some of the emotions he or she is subject to. (3) There are psychoses wherein emotional states are totally out of control.

With reference to the first group, all of us at times can get into conditions akin to physical or mental exhaustion.

There is no such thing as "mental fatigue." When we get into this condition it means there is some conflict, some area of our lives with which we cannot cope. This causes the trouble and we manifest it in the form of fatigue. It will be useful if we re-consider our attitudes to subjects manifesting conditions of extreme strain, fatigue, depression. In the past, we have thought that it would be easy to get people to "pull themselves together" and live with the problems. We have done this because we have set undue store on the physical conditions of living. We have been a little frightened of any mitigation of the physical conditions of living, of tempering the wind to the shorn lamb, because we thought there was virtue in the hard life for its own sake, or we may have thought that we would soften those under our care.

Sometimes superiors, with the best will in the world, may have withheld the sympathy they felt and the understanding they had achieved of their subjects in the mistaken idea that this was in the subjects' interest. It would be far better to allow their paternal and maternal instincts to guide them in their approach to those suffering from depressions which are within the range of normal human experience. Some superiors may have been inclined to stand by the "letter of the law" from the highest motives and have thus assumed a position of severity. If one finds that it has become necessary to mitigate the severity of the rule through frequent dispensation on the grounds that the members are overtired, this indicates the need for re-thinking the rule. If widespread and constant dispensations are necessary, the rule should be changed. If it is only one or two members who need the dispensation you can legitimately assume that the rule is not at fault. When a religious in the formative years needs constant dispensation, one ought to ask seriously whether it is reasonable to suppose he or she will be able to keep the rule for the rest of their life.

Personality Problems

A great deal might be done for people by preparing them for the inevitability of personality problems: inner conflicts, interpersonal conflicts, the sense of futility, the "awakening" of the middle years. Some of the signs mentioned earlier indicate that the problems may be becoming too great for the individual. One should know the pre-psychotic indications signalling an impending breakdown such as morbid anxiety, intolerable and prolonged depression, loss of natural adaptation, regressive behavior, paranoia, hypochondria, psychosomatic disturbances. The fact that a person is frightened, depressed, "fed-up," or tired is not itself an indication of a psychiatric problem. It may simply be an indication of a personality problem. One should look for the origins, the sources of the disturbed state. If these appear adequate, that is, sufficient to have produced the state, then one can be fairly sure that it is a personality problem. More often than not, perhaps a warm-hearted superior can resolve the problem by the most human means, genuine affection.

One should look for the defences the person is using, namely, repression of the real problem, projection, denial, rationalization. These are quite compatible with an otherwise normal personality. Sometimes the real problem is the person's inability to accept himself. Striving for misconceived perfection is a real problem. One finds that what has happened is that the person has failed to come to terms with his/her real inadequacy, with his/her changing self-image due to the passage of time, etc. More should be done to bring home to people the difference between fear and neurotic fear, perfection and "perfectionism," morbid depression and a normal sense of failure.

Perhaps the most common of personality problems is the discovery of one's own immaturity and childishness. The line of approach here should be the gradual exposing of the true weaknesses and latent strengths of the individual. Another problem is that of regression. The young woman coming into the novitiate and eventually taking vows will very often have been a fairly mature and independent person before her entering into the convent. The formation she now receives may require her to regress a little down the scale of maturity, becoming or behaving in immature ways.

Impersonal Conflicts

There are three types of conflicts with superiors: (1) the traditional type that is simply a matter of human frailty; (2) the horizontal conflict among superiors in different spheres of authority; this arises when roles are not clearly defined, for example, two different kinds of authority (superior and the principal), or two different kinds of competence (religious superior and director of the apostolate); (3) vertical conflict between generations due to lack of understanding more than to any element of ill-will.

Sometimes these conflicts, traditional, horizontal, or vertical, lead to a breakdown of interpersonal relations. Such a breakdown is a breach of charity in the spiritual sphere. On the natural plane it may produce symptoms in the form of "organic language" on the part of young religious. A member may be reasonably well-balanced and mature but in a conflict situation may slip back into behavior appropriate to a much less mature age-group. In adolescence when one wants to express something he/she does not understand, for instance, deep inner-conflict, he/she may have recourse to "organic language" such as headaches, backaches, loss of voice, appetite.

Much might be done for individuals by preparing them for the experience of tension, strain, and conflict in the middle years. Our human condition involves inner-conflicts, interpersonal conflicts with superiors and other members, a sense of failure, futility, or emptiness, and sometimes even the conviction that one has made a mistake. These are the almost inevitable phenomena of the middle years. Here then is a most important area for study. Just as one should know the indications of psychotic or neurotic conditions, so one should know that there are normal problems well within the range of normal, healthy personalities which will inevitably be met with at predictable ages.

In the early thirties, the average, normal woman, for example, will usually experience a crisis of the organism itself. One might view the organism as going through cycles. The first cycle ends at the onset of puberty; then comes the full-flowering of the organism in the early twenties; in the early thirties there occurs a crisis of tremendous organic demands in the sexual area. It may manifest itself as "malaise," unrest, insecurity, conflict with superiors, lack of insight into oneself, or as a desire for maternity. This is normal in the early thirties especially in young women who have made the sacrifice of their maternal role in the twenties. It would not be human to pass into the thirties and not experience the emptiness and lack of such maternal fulfillment, at the natural level. A strong temptation to opt out of the religious life may be expected to appear at this time.

A sense of futility is the ordinary experience of the forties, especially between forty-three and forty-seven. If we are prepared for the difficulty we are less likely to take it too seriously. If we are forearmed against it and realize that it is no indication we have made a mistake, we shall more easily "weather the storm." The experience of the early forties—futility, emptiness, etc., can be the occasion of a new conversion, a new awakening to the reality of life and the meaning of the previous twenty years or more spent as a religious. Perhaps the most common problem is the discovery of one's dependence, the realization of the limitations of one's personality. There might even be some foundation for the experience of futility and inadequacy. We do not have to face this as long as it is unknown, but when we have gone through twenty years of religious life without accomplishing what we thought we would, we may become acutely conscious of the hidden inadequacies of our personality. One then observes a "flare-up" of depression, hysteria, anxiety in the early or middle-forties and wonders why. Mostly it is because people are not prepared for the storm.

Morale

The question of morale is also an essential problem for the religious of our day. Morale is a psychological factor which depends, first, on a conviction of the worthwhileness of the end towards which one is striving. Secondly, morale is a conviction of the necessity of the means. For instance, if a person is not convinced of the necessity of binding himself by vows, he cannot succeed as a religious in the sense in which this means a binding of himself by vows. He cannot bind himself by rule unless he is convinced of the necessity of rules and even meticulous regulations. Thirdly, another constituent of morale is maximal knowledge of all the facts.

Unhappily, we seem to have weakened our morale by not recognizing the end itself very clearly; we have a clear enough model of what spiritual perfection consists of, but we do not have much of a vision of what the mature, well-informed Christian, consecrated in the religious life ought to be. We have confused spiritual perfection with concepts of immaturity. We must try to form a clear idea of the end result, the fully mature, fully formed man or woman who is also a consecrated person. This is very important to the whole question of attracting new vocations.

There is the necessity of means. We may have in the past emphasized some means which were not necessary. This was one source of confusion. The way to deal with this is the maximizing of knowledge. Superiors in religious orders still try to preserve an unnecessary secrecy all too often.

What is necessary for morale is, therefore: Maximal communication of knowledge based on the necessity of the means, which itself is related to a clear vision of the end. The question we have to ask with reference to every aspect of the religious life is: Is this of divine origin or human devising? We shall find that very little is of divine origin. Obviously the vows themselves, the obligation to pray, the evangelical counsels, are of divine origin, but the implementation of these is through ways devised by man. These means of human devising must be carefully re-appraised, asking ourselves what is the purpose of this or that particular device. The Church has had to ask what the purpose of the Eucharistic fast was. It had been taken for granted that it somehow was related to the sanctification of the Christian. As soon as the Church realized that this fast, while it did prepare many for a worthy reception of Holy Communion, was keeping many away from receiving, it changed the law. With reference to each regulation of the religious life we must ask: What is its purpose and does it attain that purpose? We have to be ready to show that every regulation is necessary and achieves its end.

Another question is: What might attain the purpose better? For instance, the regulation of recreation in communities is grounded in an historical fact. There was a time when to sit and sew and chat was recreation for young women and girls and even for mothers after putting the children to bed. Recreation is essential and its purpose is to renew the spirit, relieve persons of their tensions, etc. But does sewing and chatting achieve the purpose? For some, yes; for others, no. Is there some other way that this could be better attained?

We must ask what other purposes ought to be aimed at? What are the purposes of this community here and now? If there are other purposes, what other devices do we need to achieve them? Each successive age and culture must recreate religious life in the light of its own insights into human nature and human behavior. There are many ways in which religious life might be enriched through the insights of social psychology and occupational psychology.

Spiritual Problems

There are on the whole four kinds of spiritual problems: (1) the crisis of vocation; (2) the crisis of faith; (3) the crisis of purity; and (4) moral depression.

With women religious the crisis of vocation occurs at the point in the early thirties when organic demands are at their maximum. With men it is almost always a decade later. In the period twenty-nine to thirty-five, a woman can have a vocation problem because she knows that she could still marry and have a family. It is probable that this should be faced in clear consciousness and not be repressed. Girls in their early twenties should be told that the sacrifices they are presently making are comparatively easy, but will become more onerous and painful in their thirties. They should also be told that this storm will pass as long as they see through the storm and recognize that they have not made a mistake in their vocation. If they realized it was a passing phase that will diminish in intensity, they will not become preoccupied with the problem when it arises. If they feel they are not unique it will make it easier for them.

There is another reason why the problem becomes acute at this time. During the period of the novitiate, juniorate, college training as a teacher, nurses' training, etc., there are natural goals looming ahead which act as stimuli enabling her to give her best. There is also the experience of a new world, the possibility of exciting ways of life in a new community, perhaps even in foreign fields. These are natural motives but they are not divorced from the supernatural ones. We provide these channels in the early teens and twenties, but coming up to the termination of the twenties we seem to remove them; we seem to be unable to provide religious with new motives once they have attained their degrees or arrived at their mission. For a while they will be carried along on the crest of the wave of early motivations, but by the commencement of the thirties the vision of the future becomes a little clouded. It is as if we launched them from the late twenties to live by faith alone. This is good in itself, but St. Paul's "just man who lives by faith" is a man of great integrity and sanctity. We should not normally expect an ordinary person still in formation to live by faith alone. The strong organic demand, coupled with our failure to provide new stimuli once the natural motivations have been removed, is one of the greatest causes of precipitating personality problems.

The crisis of faith will be more frequent in the future than it has in the past. It seems to be taking on a new form in contemporary religious life and the priesthood. Whereas in the past the crisis of faith was created with regard to some particular doctrine, it is now manifesting itself about religion itself or perhaps more particularly about the value of the religious life. One hears the question, "Is there a future for the religious life?" Such questions are answered sometimes by the wrong approach, by attempting to present the utilitarian value of the religious life. We ought to recognize that if we question the value of the religious life, we are questioning the value of religion itself.

We have led many young people and some young religious to think that faith is an experiential phenomenon, something they can observe in themselves or discover through introspection. We must make more explicit to our young religious the unique character of faith as an act, a choice, or a commitment, and not as something to be discovered, resting passively within oneself. In this respect it resembles a vocation which is not something one discovers within oneself through introspection. This is the most dangerous error in the religious life at the present moment. Vocation is a response to a calling to go along a particular road, and this response is a free choice, an activity, not a passive, observable fact which one finds within oneself.

We must convey to our young religious that having a vocation or a vow of chastity is not a goal achieved or a final state of being. Repeated acts and commitments are intrinsic to their state. If a young religious in his/her early thirties gets depressed and thinks he/she has no vocation, we must be able to point out that a vocation is not a thing one has or does not have. It is a new form of loving, a new kind of doing which is obedience, both being predicated on a new kind of choosing which is sacrifice.

The crisis of purity is the most common of these personality problems. Just as a vocation has to be renewed by constant choosing, so we should teach religious that chastity intrinsically depends upon renewed acts of choosing. The virtue lies in a different kind of loving and it is not achieved by a single act of taking a vow. Sometimes the stability of the young religious is weakened by the discovery that the choice of chastity has to be renewed frequently and more so even than obedience. We ought not allow them to believe that having a problem in chastity is a counter-indication with regard to vocation. In fact, not having a problem or never having had one might be a more concrete counter-indication.

Finally, the crisis of moral depression manifests itself neither as a problem of faith nor chastity, but in a sense of the meaninglessness of prayer, the futility of mortification, the worthlessness of the future which appears as a total blank. This may indicate a minor psychiatric depression or it may indicate *acedia*. *Acedia* is a genuine spiritual trial but it may be duplicated in the natural order by moral depression. Once again expert advice is necessary. The most common way in which this appears is in sub-clinical depression or one not intense enough to demand psychiatric care. This type of depression runs along under the surface all the time, and some of its symptoms are intermittent sobbing, dependence, isolation within the community. In behavior it may present itself in a loss of interest in the Mass or religious observance. If it is not a spiritual trial, it may take months and years to overcome. The superior should not lose hope and this should be conveyed to the subject who should be reassured that provided he or she lives the religious life wholeheartedly the depression will cease of its own with time.

Suggested Remedies

We ought to learn from the world around us. The psychologist can be a great help. In industrial psychology we study the worker on the bench and the interpersonal relations in the factory. We have never done this in societies of religious men and women and yet they are social groups. We should investigate the motivation and incentives of people at different stages of the religious life and make a close study of interpersonal relations within the community. There is available to us a great deal of information about group dynamics, interaction between members of a group, and between groups. None of this has been applied to religious communities.

Secondly, we should seek out ways of urging those in their twenties to take further steps into maturation.

Thirdly, permanence and stability should be balanced against the need for and possibility of change. It might be a good idea to establish as a regular procedure that people in the middle-age group be prepared for a new kind of life and be trained in new skills. We must prepare ourselves for massive cultural change in the world around us and move even faster than the changing society in which we live, otherwise we may find ourselves by-passed by the world we ought to serve. There is no reason why we should not use all the devices for the elimination of routine work and thus release subjects for more productive work. There are all sorts of areas in which to keep new goals and incentives before people, and in this way eliminate or preclude the occurrence of many problems.